SELF-CROWNED

JOURNAL PT. II

YOUR SELF-LOVE ACTION PLAN AND ACCOUNTABILITY PARTNER.

12/4/18

CREATED BY

Derrick Jaxn

Self-Crowned Journal
ISBN: 978-0-9910336-9-0

selfcrowned.com

TABLE OF CONTENTS

WELCOME

You're in the right place. Now, let's do the right thing..
Understand that Self-Crowned is not a magic trick. It's a resource and it only works as a complementary piece to your commitment to your self-love. Also understand that each component of this journal is specifically designed to help reinforce the version of yourself that will allow you to live your most fulfilled life regardless of who is in or out of it, what money you do or do not currently have, and regardless of what past experiences convinced you that you would be broken forever.

After completing the Self-Crowned Journal, you will notice yourself holding the keys to your mental and emotional state throughout the day in moments you formerly would have turned over to whoever it was you last loved that decided to pop back up on your mind. You'll notice the frustrations that used to consume you simply don't anymore, and the people who used to drain you won't feel comfortable remaining in your presence while those looking to pour into you will be drawn to you and want to stick around long-term. This is the proven power of the exercises within these pages, but they only work if you truly commit to them.

It's time to turn your mindset around, rediscover your happiness, and attract every blessing that already has your name on it. *LET'S DO IT, TOGETHER.*

Every day, you're going to start your morning by writing out an affirmation for what it is you deserve or identify within yourself as already having as an intrinsic quality. One example may be, "I am beautiful, and it's obvious to everyone who deserves to see it." Another example would be, "I'm capable of accomplishing every goal that's been placed upon my heart." Affirmations rewrite well as your affirmation being put on full display. Allow yourself to feel the joy and gratitude of seeing those things come full circle, and even the reaction by those who will see them, too. If you've never meditated before, this may be uncomfortable at first, but the rewards are tremendous!

Entries don't have to be elaborate or perfect, but you must absolutely mean them as this will become a regular from that affirmation, follow through the rest of the page as outlined, without skipping a single portion. The meditation is most effective when your phone notifications are turned off or completely out of reach, and there's soft music to help create a peaceful atmosphere around you. The intent is to completely immerse yourself in the visualization of the materialization of the goals you wrote down as reference for the future, and possibly years to come.

After completing each week of entries, you'll then complete your weekly score card. Take the time out for yourself, no matter how busy your life is, to dedicate yourself to this as well as the rest of the journal. This is a life-changing process from the inside out, and you deserve the space to dedicate yourself to it.

SELF-CROWNED IS...

to self-love what being in shape is to exercise. It's a goal and a commitment wrapped in one, and it's reserved for those who see themselves as worth the effort regardless of what the world throws at them. You don't just go work out one day to say you did it. You do so to become healthy and fit. The same goes for self-love. You practice it with the intention of doing more than just knowing you did, but rather because you're focused on becoming self-crowned.

This concept originated several years ago when I first realized how self-love played into healthy relationships, both inwardly and outwardly. What is now for many just another trend initially found its way into my life as an emergency vest when I felt like I was drowning in the trials and tribulations that came my way.

The resources I tapped into, which claimed to reinforce the pillars of self-improvement, took me several years to find and sift through. I've read the books, attended the seminars, booked the therapy sessions (which I still highly recommend), practiced the meditations, and talked to the elders that guided me to create my own facilitator of development for others. That facilitator is what you'll find here in the form of Self-Crowned VIP, which contains my courses, blogs, live chats, Self-Crowned community, and now the Self-Crowned journal, all centered around one concept: leveling up.

The journal you're holding was first of all the Self-Crowned resources to be created and will continue to be the pillar of the transformation for those who truly commit to this process experience. It's the pseudo-boot camp that changes your entire focus for the day from whatever asked for your attention to the mission of loving yourself.

Although it takes some getting used to, the Self-Crowned journal has been simplified for the busy man and woman of today who don't have several hours of free time for journaling. The minimalistic approach allows for easy integration into even the busiest schedule yet remains effective in increasing productivity and positivity when used consistently.

However, it's also for the people who see themselves worthy of the ongoing investment. I've dedicated my life towards pouring into those types of people, which in turn, has kept me fulfilled as well, and if you're ready to take this journey to the next level of your life, then I'll have you know it's my honor and privilege to join you.

LET'S DO THIS.

Derrick Jaxn

"Once you make up in your mind that you truly deserve something, the universe will conspire to give it to you."

Derrick Jaxn

12 PILLARS OF SELF-CROWNED

OVER THE YEARS OF TEACHING AND REINFORCING THE CONCEPT OF SELF-LOVE, I'VE COME UP WITH 12 WAYS TO APPLY IT TO LIFE TO INCREASE THE AMOUNT THAT YOU HAVE FOR YOURSELF AND ATTRACT AROUND YOU.

1. GETTING BETTER SLEEP.

Benefit: To recharge your brain and body to handle the daily tasks and unexpected events that may occur throughout the day. While this accidentally happens on occasion, this should become a top priority for those looking to win their daily battles on a consistent basis.

Actions to support: Turn off all electronics at least two hours before bedtime. Vent to someone about things troubling you, with their permission. Cool your room temperature by two degrees or more. Cut off all liquids four hours prior. Take melatonin. Hang blackout curtains.

2. REMOVING TOXIC PEOPLE FROM YOUR LIFE.

Benefit: While it's beneficial to pour positivity into your life, the longer it mixes with negativity, the less your efforts will add up to a positive outcome. Sometimes the first step to living a healthier life is to simply remove those who are pouring in the poison.

Actions to support: Unfollow them on social media to decrease the frequency of them in your thoughts. On the next conversation, state your standards and don't back down. Block their number the moment they even slightly attempt to compromise your clearly stated standards. Go into the Self-Crowned app and engage with others regularly.

3. CARING LESS OF WHAT PEOPLE THINK OF YOU.

Benefit: Nothing is wrong with appreciating the love when it's shown, and it's natural to be offended sometimes at the thoughts of others, but ultimately, whatever makes you will break you, and the opinions of outsiders don't deserve that power. You have zero control over the level of understanding someone else is capable of or their intentions to genuinely try to understand you, and therefore, you should have a correlative level of zero investment into what they think.

Actions to support: Turn off notifications from social media. Post a selfie, and don't look at the comments or number of likes until the next day. Don't look at comments under anyone else's selfies either. Unfollow judgmental accounts on social media. Disengage from gossipy conversations.

4. GAINING CONFIDENCE IN MEETING NEW PEOPLE.

Benefit: To increase your net worth, you also need to increase your network. You are the company you keep. Both of these statements are well-known and accepted by those who've taken charge of their direction in life, and the same should go for you, too.

Actions to support: Compliment someone you don't know and then walk off. Ask a complete stranger for help in doing something or for an answer to a random question Go to a social environment you've never been to and make eye contact with a smile at a minimum of three people. Attend a networking event in your area even if you don't know the company hosting it. Introduce yourself to three new people in Self-Crowned.

5. DEVELOPING MORE POSITIVE THOUGHTS ABOUT YOURSELF.

Benefit: 80% of our thoughts are negative when we're unintentional about them. That has resulted in a society of people suffering from aggravated depression, anxiety, and low self-esteem, which in turn, has convinced people with the potential to lead fulfilling lives that their life will never be worth living. Increasing how kind we are to ourselves sets the tone for not only a better life but appreciating just how great it already is so we can enjoy more of it.

Actions to support: Find an affirmation from "I've Come Too Far" or "I Still Deserve It" books in the Self-Crowned app, and repeat to yourself three times throughout the day. Turn on your favorite song and dance to it naked and with a smile. Give thanks for specific details about your body, character, and talents. Spend time in deep prayer and meditation about the things you want and deserve.

6. SPENDING MONEY MORE WISELY.

Benefit: Although money is not everything, it matters, big time. Having very little tends to impact our romantic relationships, relationships with our children, and even the relationship we have with ourselves because it affects how much time we can invest into each of those areas. By spending more wisely, you not only can increase the luxuries of life you get to enjoy from time to time, but most importantly, you give yourself more time to spend with the people who matter because you don't have to be dedicated to constantly trying to get out of debt.

Actions to support: Write down every dollar you spent yesterday, and cut out anything that's not absolutely necessary. Immediately take money out of your account, put it in your closet where it's difficult to reach and you can't see, and don't touch it. Cook instead of going out to eat. Overhaul your home for any loose change you can find. Use natural lights in your home until nighttime. Cut off AC/heat when you're not at home. Set up a payment plan for your biggest credit card debt.

7. BEING MORE SELFISH.

Benefit: You can't pour from an empty cup, and when you maintain a healthy level of selfishness, you never will have to. Your life can't revolve around helping others for long if there's not a reservoir of investment you have for yourself in case others aren't always as reciprocal as they should be, which will happen. So, being selfish is not only a safety measure, it's common sense when done correctly.

Actions to support: Tell someone who asks you for something, "No" or "Not right now" at least once, today. Spend 30 minutes getting away from everything, and take no phone calls/texts. Set an hour aside every day. Identify a commitment you've made that doesn't sit right with you, and kindly let the person know you can no longer oblige.

8. LETTING YOUR GUARD DOWN ON PURPOSE.

Benefit: Your guard is for protecting yourself from those who haven't earned the privilege of coming inside. Loving someone fully requires you to be able to open up, and so does relating to people who've been through similar experiences as you. When we get hurt, we naturally resort to putting our guard up and never again wanting it to come down, but finding the balance between when to be vulnerable and when not to be allows for the duality of being both protected and ready to be loved in the way you deserve.

Actions to support: Go into the Self-Crowned app and start a thread on something very personal to you. Call someone you love and ask them if they have a moment so you can tell them why you love them. Write down on a piece of paper all of the people and respective ways they've hurt you.

9. GETTING MORE PHYSICAL ACTIVITY.

Benefit: Beyond just the obvious value of living longer and with less health issues, getting physical activity can increase your self-esteem and build habits of winning small battles even on days you don't feel like it. The progress you see physically will motivate you to see progress in other areas of your life and may even inspire others around you to do the same.

Actions to support: Park in the furthest place from the location you've driven to. Take an additional 15 minutes before work to walk down the street from your house and back. Get a local gym membership and sign up for a fitness class that fits in your schedule.

10. EATING HEALTHIER.

NO JUNK FOOD. NO ALCOHOL. DRINK A GALLON OF WATER. EAT AN ADDITIONAL SALAD. SUBSTITUTE FRIED OPTIONS FOR SOMETHING GRILLED OR BAKED.

11. BEING MORE APPRECIATIVE.

Benefit: It's not a huge surprise to anyone that we won't live forever. It's also not a huge surprise that as short as life seems, we'll outlast many of the things we see around us today, and there's no telling how long we have with those we love. Unfortunately our subconscious doesn't know that. It gets so used to things that it's not until we lose them that we realize their value in our lives, unless, of course, we're intentional about appreciating them now. Being more appreciative of what we have now removes the regret so many feel later that they didn't do so when they had the chance and increases the fulfillment of your day-to-day life because you're purposely aware of the ways your life is already awesome.

Actions to support: Journaling. Counting your blessings every night. Blocking out time to invest in your friendships and relationships every day. Limiting the time you spend on your phone when in the presence of family and friends. Coupling every complaint with a reason to also be thankful.

12. HELPING OTHERS.

Benefit: Self-Crowned is not strictly about living for yourself, but even if it was, it would include the way that you coexist with others, especially those that pour into you. But most importantly, we were put on this Earth in part to be of help to our fellow human, and we were all equipped with the ability to do so whether it be in a major way for millions of people or in some small but meaningful way to a few. Helping others will not only allow you to fulfill that responsibility, but will also increase the value you feel to this world which is a basic human need for high self-esteem.

Actions to support: Feeding the homeless. Taking spare change and investing into Gofundme causes near and dear to your heart. Shouting out a small business on your social media. Giving socks and t-shirts to the homeless during the colder months. Helping raise money for cancer awareness groups.

SELF-CROWNED COMMITMENT

THE SELF-CROWNED COMMITMENT IS EXACTLY WHAT IT SOUNDS LIKE; YOU MAKING A DECLARATION TO LOVE YOURSELF BETTER THAN YOU HAVE BEEN IN THE PAST. BE CLEAR. BE SPECIFIC. CHOOSE THE THREE AREAS OF YOUR LIFE YOU KNOW YOU NEED TO FOCUS ON AND HOW YOU'RE GOING TO GO ABOUT FOCUSING ON THEM WITH A SIGNATURE AND DATE SO YOU KNOW IT'S REAL. FROM THERE, IT'S TIME TO MAKE IT HAPPEN.

WHAT THREE AREAS OF YOUR LIFE NEED WORK THE MOST? CHOOSE THOSE.

OVER THE NEXT 13 WEEKS, I WILL BETTER MY LIFE BY ◯ GETTING BETTER SLEEP. ✸ REMOVING TOXIC PEOPLE FROM MY LIFE. ◯ CARING LESS OF WHAT PEOPLE THINK OF ME. ◯ HAVING MORE CONFIDENCE IN MEETING NEW PEOPLE.

◯ BEING MORE SELFISH. ◯ THINKING MORE HIGHLY OF MYSELF. ✸ SPENDING MONEY MORE WISELY. ◯ LETTING MY GUARD DOWN. ◯ GETTING MORE ACTIVE. ✸ EATING HEALTHIER. ◯ BEING MORE ORGANIZED. ◯ BEING MORE APPRECIATIVE. ◯ HELPING OTHERS. ◯ OTHER_____

_____ (MAX OF THREE)

WHAT IS YOUR WHY FOR DOING THIS? WRITE THAT HERE.

IT'S IMPORTANT FOR ME TO IMPROVE MY LIFE IN THESE AREAS BECAUSE_____ My children are watching me as an example of how they should live their life, and I don't want to pass down generational curses that were passed down to me.

YOUR FIRST AREA FOR IMPROVEMENT THAT YOU CHOSE ABOVE'S GAME PLAN.

I commit to _Removing toxic people_ by completing the following three tasks _once_ a day at least __ two __ day(s) a week from week _1_ to week _4_ .

1. _Unfollowing people online that constantly spew negativity_
2. _Blocking exes and former flames who only want one thing_
3. _Standing firm on my principles regardless who it offends_

YOUR SECOND AREA FOR IMPROVEMENT THAT YOU CHOSE ABOVE'S GAME PLAN.

I commit to _Spending money wisely_ by completing the following three tasks _once_ a day at least __ five __ day(s) a week from week _1_ to week _4_ .

1. _Unfollowing people online that constantly spew negativity_
2. _Blocking exes and former flames who only want one thing_
3. _Standing firm on my principles regardless who it offends_

YOUR THIRD AREA FOR IMPROVEMENT THAT YOU CHOSE ABOVE'S GAME PLAN.

I commit to _Eating healthier_ by completing the following three tasks _once_ a day at least __ five __ day(s) a week from week _10_ to week _13_ .

1. _Substituting all fried options for grilled or baked_
2. _Fasting from alcohol, completely_
3. _Cooking instead of eating out for breakfast and dinner_

AS I COMPLETE EACH OF MY SELF-CROWNED GOALS, I WILL REWARD MYSELF BY _Taking an entire day to myself for a spa appointment, date, and time spent in my bubble bath_

_____ .

I will do the following things to ensure I fully utilize my Self-Crowned journal and Self-Crowned VIP community to help me achieve my goals:

1. _Make a morning habit of checking new posts and writing in my journal each day._
2. _Getting an accountability partner from Self-Crowned who will take this journey with me._
3. _Set reminders in my phone to ensure I remember ._

I deserve these transformations in my life because I am ____loyal____ , ____trustworthy____ , and ____God-fearing____ .

Name: _Derrick Jaxn_   Date: _Sep. 21st 2019_   Signature: _Derrick Jaxn_

"*Real friends see you surpass them in life and continue cheering for you because it was never a competition to begin with.*"

Derrick Jaxn

SELF-CROWNED CALENDAR

THE SELF-CROWNED CALENDAR IS YOUR SPACE TO KEEP A TOP-LEVEL LIST OF THINGS YOU WANT TO GET DONE THROUGHOUT THE MONTH. YOUR LIFE DOESN'T STOP JUST BECAUSE YOU'RE PERSONALLY TRANSFORMING, AND IT SHOULDN'T HAVE TO. SO, STAY ON TRACK WITH THE REST OF YOUR LIFE BY JOTTING DOWN IMPORTANT EVENTS, MEETINGS, OR JUST THINGS TO KEEP IN MIND FROM A MACRO LEVEL.

DON'T OVERTHINK. UNDERTHINK. TAKE THE STRESS OF TRYING TO REMEMBER OFF YOUR HANDS BY JOTTING DOWN WEEKLY TASKS IN YOUR MONTHLY CALENDAR.

MONTH: September

S	M	T	W
Brunch with the girls Begin Self-Crowned Journal		Hubby's B-DAY	1st Pilates Class
	Micro-Needling appt		
Check-in with accountability partner		Whole Foods coupons expire	
			Lacey's Basketball Game
	Order mom & dad anniversary gift		

DAILY ENTRY

WE'VE SIMPLIFIED THE TIME YOU SPEND IN YOUR JOURNAL EVERY DAY SO YOU CAN SPEND MOST OF YOUR TIME FOCUSING ON THE ACTION STEPS TOWARDS LOVING YOU. HOWEVER, THE DAILY ENTRIES ONLY WORK IF YOU MAKE TIME FOR THEM AND FILL THEM OUT PROPERLY STARTING WITH THE FOCUS OF THE DAY AND HOW YOU'RE GOING TO GO ABOUT EXECUTING ON IMPROVING IN THAT FOCUS AREA.

FROM THERE YOU SIMPLY RETURN AT NIGHT TO SPEAK ON THE WAYS IN WHICH YOU WON AS IT RELATES TO THAT FOCUS AND WHAT YOU WANT TO IMPROVE ON GOING FORWARD, ENDING ON THE WAYS THAT THE UNIVERSE IS ALIGNING THE THINGS YOU CAN'T CONTROL IN YOUR FAVOR.

WEEK 1 | DAY 1

WHAT IS THE AREA OF FOCUS FOR THIS WEEK?

Today's Self-Crowned Focus: _Removing toxic people from my life_

Actions to take:

Unfollowing all negative accounts

Standing firm on my principles

Nightly Check-In:

BRAG A LITTLE. YOU DID THAT!

Wins(How did you crush it today?):
- unfollowed @celebdramaweluv, @mgtowhg and @loveanddysfunctionrealitytv
- Was able to converse with my mom about the respect my spouse deserves
- Refused a date offer from a guy who'd previously hit on my best friend

NOTHING WRONG WITH MAKING MISTAKES, BUT LET'S ADDRESS THEM.

Lessons Learned(Opportunities for improvement?):

Was a little too hard on my coworker who honestly didn't mean to take my parking spot

Didn't let hubby finish his sentences today about how work went for him

REMIND YOURSELF HOW THE UNIVERSE IS ON YOUR SIDE.

Three blessings you can count(Things completely out of your control that went your way):

1. _I made it to work and back today safely_

2. _I have absolutely no symptoms of any life-threatening diseases_

3. _My home was fully intact with no signs of break-ins when I got home today_

WEEKLY SCORE CARD

EVERY WEEK, KEEP YOURSELF ACCOUNTABLE FOR HOW WELL YOU STUCK TO THE PLAN THAT YOU SET IN THE 13-WEEK SELF-CROWNED COMMITMENT. LOOK FROM A MACRO LEVEL AT WHAT COULD'VE BEEN BETTER OR WHAT YOU DID THAT EXCEEDED YOUR EXPECTATIONS SO YOU CAN CONTINUE ON THE RIGHT PATH. DOING THESE REFLECTIONS WILL ALLOW YOU TO BOTH IMPROVE AT SELF-IMPROVING AS WELL AS APPRECIATE THE EFFORT YOU'RE INVESTING INTO YOURSELF FOR A MUCH DESERVED PAT ON THE BACK.

WHAT IS THE AREA OF FOCUS FOR THIS WEEK?

Focus   _Removing toxic people from my life_

Actions Taken	SUN	MON	TUES	WED	THURS	FRI	SAT	TOTAL
Unfollowing all negative accounts	X	X		X	X		X	5/7
Standing firm on my principles	X	X	X	X	X	X	X	7/7
Blocking Exes					X	X		2/7
							SUM TOTAL	14/21

Looking at your totals for the week, does it reflect your absolute best effort to have improved in your focus area?   _YES!_

Out of all the actions, which one helped you the most?

Standing on my principles(and it felt good!)

What are you most proud of yourself for so far?

That this time I actually stuck to my plan. I didn't get distracted or frustrated. I held on for an entire week, and that's rare, but it won't be anymore.

Realistically, and with your absolute best effort, what do you believe your total sum total will be next week, and how will you achieve this?

Definitely able to match this with my best effort. I gave this one everything and I'm pleased with the results. Already fired up for the next week!

FREE WRITE

YOU'LL NOTICE A LOT OF BLANK PAGES IN THIS JOURNAL. WELL, DON'T LEAVE THEM THAT WAY. THOSE ARE THE FREE WRITE PAGES DESIGNED TO GIVE YOU SPACE TO MAKE FREE EXPRESSION A PART OF YOUR LIFE WHETHER IT WAS BEFORE OR NOT. TRY IT, IT'S GOOD FOR YOU.

VENT. GOOD, BAD, AND UGLY. THE ONLY RULE HERE IS TRANSPARENCY.

FREE WRITE:

It's not easy staying encouraged, but I'm trying. I'm realizing that there are so many people who aren't going to be able to come to this next phase in my life and although it's supposed to be that way, it's still scary. I do feel better knowing that Ronnie fully supports me and even offered to join me in my Self-Crowned journey, so that's a good sign. I even think I saw Kaleb eyeing my journal, so maybe it can be an entire family affair. Lol Maybe not, idk. We'll see. For now, I'm just excited and afraid all at once at what's to come but I refuse to back down. This is it. This is my chance to finally take control of my life on a personal level and I won't let it slip through my hands this time. Nope. Not this time.

REMINDER: IF YOU'RE ABLE TO READ THIS, THAT MEANS YOU STILL HAVE A PURPOSE OVER YOUR LIFE AND EVERYTHING WITHIN YOU THAT'S NEEDED TO MANIFEST IT.

SELF-CROWNED HACKS

PUT YOUR JOURNAL ON YOUR NIGHTSTAND OR UNDER YOUR PILLOW, SOMEWHERE YOU CAN'T AVOID SEEING IT BEFORE YOU GO TO SLEEP.

DEVELOP THE HABIT OF JOURNALING BY ATTACHING IT TO ANOTHER HABIT YOU HAVE EVERY DAY. FOR EXAMPLE, IF MORNING PRAYER IS A HABIT, JOURNAL EVERY DAY RIGHT BEFORE OR AFTER PRAYER.

RESIST THE URGE TO FEEL AWKWARD FOR JOURNALING. ALTHOUGH IT ISN'T WILDLY POPULAR FOR THE PURPOSE YOU'RE DOING IT, NEITHER IS THE GOAL YOU'RE GOING TO ACHIEVE BY DOING IT.

APOLOGIZE TO NO ONE IF HOW THEY "FEEL" IS THE ONLY PROBLEM WITH YOU BECOMING A BETTER VERSION OF YOU. THANK THEM FOR UNDERSTANDING AND OFFER NO JUDGMENT IF THEY DON'T, BUT NEVER APOLOGIZE!

DON'T STOP WHEN THE JOURNAL STOPS. THIS IS A LIFELONG JOURNEY FOR EVERYONE, INCLUDING THOSE ALREADY LIVING THEIR BEST LIVES. THE SELF-CROWNED JOURNAL WILL GET YOU HEADED IN THE RIGHT DIRECTION AND GIVE YOU GUIDANCE, BUT UNDERSTAND, THE WORK HAS JUST BEGUN!

SELF-CROWNED COMMITMENT

OVER THE NEXT 13 WEEKS, I WILL BETTER MY LIFE BY ◯ GETTING BETTER SLEEP. ◯ REMOVING TOXIC PEOPLE FROM MY LIFE. ◯ CARING LESS OF WHAT PEOPLE THINK OF ME. ◯ HAVING MORE CONFIDENCE IN MEETING NEW PEOPLE.

◯ BEING MORE SELFISH. ◯ THINKING MORE HIGHLY OF MYSELF. ◯ SPENDING MONEY MORE WISELY. ◯ LETTING MY GUARD DOWN. ◯ GETTING MORE ACTIVE. ◯ EATING HEALTHIER. ◯ BEING MORE ORGANIZED. ◯ BEING MORE APPRECIATIVE. ◯ HELPING OTHERS. ◯ OTHER_____

_____ (MAX OF THREE)

IT'S IMPORTANT FOR ME TO IMPROVE MY LIFE IN THESE AREAS BECAUSE _____

_____

_____

YOUR FIRST AREA FOR IMPROVEMENT THAT YOU CHOSE ABOVE'S GAME PLAN.

I commit to _____ by completing the following three tasks _____ a day at least _____ day(s) a week from week _____ to week _____ :

1. _____

2. _____

3. _____

YOUR SECOND AREA FOR IMPROVEMENT THAT YOU CHOSE ABOVE'S GAME PLAN.

I commit to _____ by completing the following three tasks _____ a day at least _____ day(s) a week from week _____ to week _____ :

1. _____

2. _____

3. _____

YOUR THIRD AREA FOR IMPROVEMENT THAT YOU CHOSE ABOVE'S GAME PLAN.

I commit to _____ by completing the following three tasks _____ a day at least _____ day(s) a week from week _____ to week _____ :

1. _____

2. _____

3. _____

AS I COMPLETE EACH OF MY SELF-CROWNED GOALS, I WILL REWARD MYSELF BY _____

_____

_____.

I will do the following things to ensure I fully utilize my Self-Crowned journal and Self-Crowned VIP community to help me achieve my goals:

1. _____

2. _____

3. _____

I deserve these transformations in my life because I am _____, _____, and

_____.

Name: _____ Date: _____ Signature: _____

"Real friends see you surpass them in life and continue cheering for you because it was never a competition to begin with."

Derrick Jaxn

MONTH:

S	M	T	W

MONTH:

T	F	S	

"You'll never have everyone's approval, so it's best to focus on your own."

Derrick Jaxn

"There's nothing like a woman who takes too much pride in herself to remain in the company of those who disrespect her."

Derrick Jaxn

MONTH:

S	M	T	W

MONTH:

T	F	S	

"Give up on anyone who leaves you fighting for the two of you by yourself."

Derrick Jaxn

"You can't deny what's consistent. You can't trust what's not."

Derrick Jaxn

MONTH:

S	M	T	W

MONTH:

T	F	S	

WEEK 1 | DAY 1

Today's Self-Crowned Focus: _____

Actions to take:

_____

_____

_____

_____

_____

_____

Nightly Check-In:

BRAG A LITTLE. YOU DID THAT!

Wins(How did you crush it today?):

_____

_____

_____

_____

NOTHING WRONG WITH MAKING MISTAKES, BUT LET'S ADDRESS THEM.

Lessons Learned(Opportunities for improvement?):

_____

_____

_____

_____

REMIND YOURSELF HOW THE UNIVERSE IS ON YOUR SIDE.

Three blessings you can count(Things completely out of your control that went your way):

1. _____

_____

2. _____

_____

3. _____

_____

FREE WRITE:

_____

_____

_____

_____

_____

_____

_____

_____

_____

_____

_____

_____

_____

_____

_____

_____

_____

_____

_____

_____

_____

_____

_____

_____

_____

_____

_____

_____

_____

_____

_____

REMINDER: IF YOU'RE ABLE TO READ THIS, THAT MEANS YOU STILL HAVE A PURPOSE OVER YOUR LIFE AND EVERYTHING WITHIN YOU THAT'S NEEDED TO MANIFEST IT.

WEEK 1 | DAY 2

Today's Self-Crowned Focus: _____

Actions to take:

_____

_____

_____

_____

_____

_____

Nightly Check-In:

Wins(How did you crush it today?):

_____

_____

_____

_____

Lessons Learned(Opportunities for improvement?):

_____

_____

_____

_____

Three blessings you can count(Things completely out of your control that went your way):

1. _____

2. _____

3. _____

FREE WRITE:

_____
_____
_____
_____
_____
_____
_____
_____
_____
_____
_____
_____
_____
_____
_____
_____
_____
_____
_____
_____
_____
_____
_____
_____
_____
_____
_____
_____
_____
_____
_____
_____

REMINDER: IF YOU'RE ABLE TO READ THIS, THAT MEANS YOU STILL HAVE A PURPOSE OVER YOUR LIFE AND EVERYTHING WITHIN YOU THAT'S NEEDED TO MANIFEST IT.

WEEK 1 | DAY 3

Today's Self-Crowned Focus: _____

Actions to take:

_____
_____
_____
_____
_____
_____

Nightly Check-In:

Wins(How did you crush it today?):

_____
_____
_____
_____

Lessons Learned(Opportunities for improvement?):

_____
_____
_____
_____

Three blessings you can count(Things completely out of your control that went your way):

1. _____

2. _____

3. _____

FREE WRITE:

_____
_____
_____
_____
_____
_____
_____
_____
_____
_____
_____
_____
_____
_____
_____
_____
_____
_____
_____
_____
_____
_____
_____
_____
_____
_____
_____
_____
_____
_____
_____
_____
_____

REMINDER: IF YOU'RE ABLE TO READ THIS, THAT MEANS YOU STILL HAVE A PURPOSE OVER YOUR LIFE AND EVERYTHING WITHIN YOU THAT'S NEEDED TO MANIFEST IT.

WEEK 1 | DAY 4

Today's Self-Crowned Focus: _____

Actions to take:

_____

_____

_____

_____

_____

_____

Nightly Check-In:

Wins(How did you crush it today?):

_____

_____

_____

_____

Lessons Learned(Opportunities for improvement?):

_____

_____

_____

_____

Three blessings you can count(Things completely out of your control that went your way):

1. _____

_____

2. _____

_____

3. _____

_____

FREE WRITE:

_____

_____

_____

_____

_____

_____

_____

_____

_____

_____

_____

_____

_____

_____

_____

_____

_____

_____

_____

_____

_____

_____

_____

_____

_____

_____

_____

_____

_____

_____

_____

_____

_____

REMINDER: IF YOU'RE ABLE TO READ THIS, THAT MEANS YOU STILL HAVE A PURPOSE OVER YOUR LIFE AND EVERYTHING WITHIN YOU THAT'S NEEDED TO MANIFEST IT.

WEEK 1 | DAY 5

Today's Self-Crowned Focus: _____

Actions to take:

_____
_____
_____
_____
_____
_____

Nightly Check-In:

Wins(How did you crush it today?):

_____
_____
_____
_____

Lessons Learned(Opportunities for improvement?):

_____
_____
_____
_____

Three blessings you can count(Things completely out of your control that went your way):

1. _____

2. _____

3. _____

FREE WRITE:

_____
_____
_____
_____
_____
_____
_____
_____
_____
_____
_____
_____
_____
_____
_____
_____
_____
_____
_____
_____
_____
_____
_____
_____
_____
_____
_____
_____
_____
_____
_____

REMINDER: IF YOU'RE ABLE TO READ THIS, THAT MEANS YOU STILL HAVE A PURPOSE OVER YOUR LIFE AND EVERYTHING WITHIN YOU THAT'S NEEDED TO MANIFEST IT.

WEEK 1 | DAY 6

Today's Self-Crowned Focus: _____

Actions to take:

_____
_____
_____
_____
_____
_____

Nightly Check-In:

Wins(How did you crush it today?):

_____
_____
_____
_____

Lessons Learned(Opportunities for improvement?):

_____
_____
_____
_____

Three blessings you can count(Things completely out of your control that went your way):

1. _____

2. _____

3. _____

FREE WRITE:

_____
_____
_____
_____
_____
_____
_____
_____
_____
_____
_____
_____
_____
_____
_____
_____
_____
_____
_____
_____
_____
_____
_____
_____
_____
_____
_____
_____
_____
_____
_____
_____
_____

REMINDER: IF YOU'RE ABLE TO READ THIS, THAT MEANS YOU STILL HAVE A PURPOSE OVER YOUR LIFE AND EVERYTHING WITHIN YOU THAT'S NEEDED TO MANIFEST IT.

WEEK 1 | DAY 7

Today's Self-Crowned Focus: _____

Actions to take:

_____

_____

_____

_____

_____

_____

Nightly Check-In:

Wins(How did you crush it today?):

_____

_____

_____

_____

Lessons Learned(Opportunities for improvement?):

_____

_____

_____

_____

Three blessings you can count(Things completely out of your control that went your way):

1. _____

2. _____

3. _____

FREE WRITE:

_____

_____

_____

_____

_____

_____

_____

_____

_____

_____

_____

_____

_____

_____

_____

_____

_____

_____

_____

_____

_____

_____

_____

_____

_____

_____

_____

_____

_____

_____

_____

_____

_____

REMINDER: IF YOU'RE ABLE TO READ THIS, THAT MEANS YOU STILL HAVE A PURPOSE OVER YOUR LIFE AND EVERYTHING WITHIN YOU THAT'S NEEDED TO MANIFEST IT.

WEEK 1 SCORE CARD

Focus _____

Actions Taken	SUN	MON	TUES	WED	THURS	FRI	SAT	TOTAL
						SUM TOTAL		

Looking at your totals for the week, does it reflect your absolute best effort to have improved in your focus area? _____

Out of all the actions, which one helped you the most?
_____

What are you most proud of yourself for so far?
_____
_____
_____

Realistically, and with your absolute best effort, what do you believe your total sum total will be next week, and how will you achieve this?
_____
_____
_____

FREE WRITE:

_____
_____
_____
_____
_____
_____
_____
_____
_____
_____
_____
_____
_____
_____
_____
_____
_____
_____
_____
_____
_____
_____
_____
_____
_____
_____
_____
_____
_____
_____
_____
_____
_____

REMINDER: IF YOU'RE ABLE TO READ THIS, THAT MEANS YOU STILL HAVE A PURPOSE OVER YOUR LIFE AND EVERYTHING WITHIN YOU THAT'S NEEDED TO MANIFEST IT.

"If you look back five or ten years ago and cringe at the way you talked, thought, or carried yourself then don't be ashamed because that means you've grown."

Derrick Jaxn

"Protecting your energy is the number one form of self-care."

Derrick Jaxn

WEEK 2 | DAY 1

Today's Self-Crowned Focus: _____

Actions to take:

_____
_____
_____
_____
_____
_____

Nightly Check-In:

BRAG A LITTLE. YOU DID THAT!

Wins(How did you crush it today?):

_____
_____
_____
_____

NOTHING WRONG WITH MAKING MISTAKES, BUT LET'S ADDRESS THEM.

Lessons Learned(Opportunities for improvement?):

_____
_____
_____
_____

REMIND YOURSELF HOW THE UNIVERSE IS ON YOUR SIDE.

Three blessings you can count(Things completely out of your control that went your way):

1. _____
_____

2. _____
_____

3. _____
_____

WEEK 2 | DAY 1

Today's Self-Crowned Focus: _____

Actions to take:

_____
_____
_____
_____

Nightly Check-In:

_____
_____

BRAG A LITTLE. YOU DID THAT!

Wins(How did you crush it today?):

_____
_____
_____
_____

NOTHING WRONG WITH MAKING MISTAKES, BUT LET'S ADDRESS THEM.

Lessons Learned(Opportunities for improvement?):

_____
_____
_____
_____

REMIND YOURSELF HOW THE UNIVERSE IS ON YOUR SIDE.

Three blessings you can count(Things completely out of your control that went your way):

1. _____

2. _____

3. _____

FREE WRITE:

_____
_____
_____
_____
_____
_____
_____
_____
_____
_____
_____
_____
_____
_____
_____
_____
_____
_____
_____
_____
_____
_____
_____
_____
_____
_____
_____
_____
_____
_____
_____
_____

REMINDER: IF YOU'RE ABLE TO READ THIS, THAT MEANS YOU STILL HAVE A PURPOSE OVER YOUR LIFE AND EVERYTHING WITHIN YOU THAT'S NEEDED TO MANIFEST IT.

WEEK 2 | DAY 2

Today's Self-Crowned Focus: _____

Actions to take:

_____
_____
_____
_____
_____
_____

Nightly Check-In:

BRAG A LITTLE. YOU DID THAT!

Wins(How did you crush it today?):

_____
_____
_____
_____

NOTHING WRONG WITH MAKING MISTAKES, BUT LET'S ADDRESS THEM.

Lessons Learned(Opportunities for improvement?):

_____
_____
_____
_____

REMIND YOURSELF HOW THE UNIVERSE IS ON YOUR SIDE.

Three blessings you can count(Things completely out of your control that went your way):

1. _____

2. _____

3. _____

FREE WRITE:

_____
_____
_____
_____
_____
_____
_____
_____
_____
_____
_____
_____
_____
_____
_____
_____
_____
_____
_____
_____
_____
_____
_____
_____
_____
_____
_____
_____
_____
_____
_____
_____

REMINDER: IF YOU'RE ABLE TO READ THIS, THAT MEANS YOU STILL HAVE A PURPOSE OVER YOUR LIFE AND EVERYTHING WITHIN YOU THAT'S NEEDED TO MANIFEST IT.

WEEK 2 | DAY 3

Today's Self-Crowned Focus: _____

Actions to take:

_____

_____

_____

_____

_____

_____

Nightly Check-In:

BRAG A LITTLE. YOU DID THAT!

Wins(How did you crush it today?):

_____

_____

_____

_____

NOTHING WRONG WITH MAKING MISTAKES, BUT LET'S ADDRESS THEM.

Lessons Learned(Opportunities for improvement?):

_____

_____

_____

_____

REMIND YOURSELF HOW THE UNIVERSE IS ON YOUR SIDE.

Three blessings you can count(Things completely out of your control that went your way):

1. _____

2. _____

3. _____

FREE WRITE:

_____
_____
_____
_____
_____
_____
_____
_____
_____
_____
_____
_____
_____
_____
_____
_____
_____
_____
_____
_____
_____
_____
_____
_____
_____
_____
_____
_____
_____
_____
_____
_____

REMINDER: IF YOU'RE ABLE TO READ THIS, THAT MEANS YOU STILL HAVE A PURPOSE OVER YOUR LIFE AND EVERYTHING WITHIN YOU THAT'S NEEDED TO MANIFEST IT.

WEEK 2 | DAY 4

Today's Self-Crowned Focus: _____

Actions to take:

_____

_____

_____

_____

_____

_____

Nightly Check-In:

Wins(How did you crush it today?):

_____

_____

_____

_____

Lessons Learned(Opportunities for improvement?):

_____

_____

_____

_____

Three blessings you can count(Things completely out of your control that went your way):

1. _____

2. _____

3. _____

FREE WRITE:

_____
_____
_____
_____
_____
_____
_____
_____
_____
_____
_____
_____
_____
_____
_____
_____
_____
_____
_____
_____
_____
_____
_____
_____
_____
_____
_____
_____
_____
_____
_____
_____
_____

REMINDER: IF YOU'RE ABLE TO READ THIS, THAT MEANS YOU STILL HAVE A PURPOSE OVER YOUR LIFE AND EVERYTHING WITHIN YOU THAT'S NEEDED TO MANIFEST IT.

WEEK 2 | DAY 5

Today's Self-Crowned Focus: _____

Actions to take:

_____
_____
_____
_____
_____
_____

Nightly Check-In:

BRAG A LITTLE. YOU DID THAT!

Wins(How did you crush it today?):

_____
_____
_____
_____

NOTHING WRONG WITH MAKING MISTAKES, BUT LET'S ADDRESS THEM.

Lessons Learned(Opportunities for improvement?):

_____
_____
_____
_____

REMIND YOURSELF HOW THE UNIVERSE IS ON YOUR SIDE.

Three blessings you can count(Things completely out of your control that went your way):

1. _____

2. _____

3. _____

FREE WRITE:

_____
_____
_____
_____
_____
_____
_____
_____
_____
_____
_____
_____
_____
_____
_____
_____
_____
_____
_____
_____
_____
_____
_____
_____
_____
_____
_____
_____
_____
_____
_____

REMINDER: IF YOU'RE ABLE TO READ THIS, THAT MEANS YOU STILL HAVE A PURPOSE OVER YOUR LIFE AND EVERYTHING WITHIN YOU THAT'S NEEDED TO MANIFEST IT.

WEEK 2 | DAY 6

Today's Self-Crowned Focus: _____

Actions to take:

_____
_____
_____
_____
_____
_____

Nightly Check-In:

Wins(How did you crush it today?):

_____
_____
_____
_____

Lessons Learned(Opportunities for improvement?):

_____
_____
_____
_____

Three blessings you can count(Things completely out of your control that went your way):

1. _____

2. _____

3. _____

FREE WRITE:

_____
_____
_____
_____
_____
_____
_____
_____
_____
_____
_____
_____
_____
_____
_____
_____
_____
_____
_____
_____
_____
_____
_____
_____
_____
_____
_____
_____
_____
_____

REMINDER: IF YOU'RE ABLE TO READ THIS, THAT MEANS YOU STILL HAVE A PURPOSE OVER YOUR LIFE AND EVERYTHING WITHIN YOU THAT'S NEEDED TO MANIFEST IT.

WEEK 2 | DAY 7

Today's Self-Crowned Focus: _____

Actions to take:

_____
_____
_____
_____
_____
_____

Nightly Check-In:

BRAG A LITTLE. YOU DID THAT!

Wins(How did you crush it today?):

_____
_____
_____
_____

NOTHING WRONG WITH MAKING MISTAKES, BUT LET'S ADDRESS THEM.

Lessons Learned(Opportunities for improvement?):

_____
_____
_____
_____

REMIND YOURSELF HOW THE UNIVERSE IS ON YOUR SIDE.

Three blessings you can count(Things completely out of your control that went your way):

1. _____

2. _____

3. _____

FREE WRITE:

_____
_____
_____
_____
_____
_____
_____
_____
_____
_____
_____
_____
_____
_____
_____
_____
_____
_____
_____
_____
_____
_____
_____
_____
_____
_____
_____
_____
_____
_____
_____
_____

REMINDER: IF YOU'RE ABLE TO READ THIS, THAT MEANS YOU STILL HAVE A PURPOSE OVER YOUR LIFE AND EVERYTHING WITHIN YOU THAT'S NEEDED TO MANIFEST IT.

WEEK 2 SCORE CARD

Focus _____

Actions Taken

	SUN	MON	TUES	WED	THURS	FRI	SAT	TOTAL
						SUM TOTAL		

Looking at your totals for the week, does it reflect your absolute best effort to have improved in your focus area? _____

Out of all the actions, which one helped you the most?

_____

What are you most proud of yourself for so far?

_____

_____

_____

Realistically, and with your absolute best effort, what do you believe your total sum total will be next week, and how will you achieve this?

_____

_____

_____

FREE WRITE:

_____
_____
_____
_____
_____
_____
_____
_____
_____
_____
_____
_____
_____
_____
_____
_____
_____
_____
_____
_____
_____
_____
_____
_____
_____
_____
_____
_____
_____
_____
_____
_____
_____

_REMINDER: IF YOU'RE ABLE TO READ THIS, THAT MEANS YOU STILL HAVE A PURPOSE
OVER YOUR LIFE AND EVERYTHING WITHIN YOU THAT'S NEEDED TO MANIFEST IT._

"You have no obligation to sacrifice your mental health to continuously be a listening ear to someone's issues who won't do anything about them."

Derrick Jaxn

"Those who are threatened by your growth will always fault you for their inability to grow with you."

Derrick Jaxn

WEEK 3 | DAY 1

Today's Self-Crowned Focus: _____

Actions to take:

_____

_____

_____

_____

_____

_____

Nightly Check-In:

Wins(How did you crush it today?):

_____

_____

_____

_____

Lessons Learned(Opportunities for improvement?):

_____

_____

_____

_____

Three blessings you can count(Things completely out of your control that went your way):

1. _____

2. _____

3. _____

FREE WRITE:

_____

_____

_____

_____

_____

_____

_____

_____

_____

_____

_____

_____

_____

_____

_____

_____

_____

_____

_____

_____

_____

_____

_____

_____

_____

_____

_____

_____

_____

_____

_____

_____

REMINDER: IF YOU'RE ABLE TO READ THIS, THAT MEANS YOU STILL HAVE A PURPOSE OVER YOUR LIFE AND EVERYTHING WITHIN YOU THAT'S NEEDED TO MANIFEST IT.

WEEK 3 | DAY 2

Today's Self-Crowned Focus: _____

Actions to take:

_____
_____
_____
_____
_____
_____

Nightly Check-In:

Wins(How did you crush it today?):

_____
_____
_____
_____

Lessons Learned(Opportunities for improvement?):

_____
_____
_____
_____

Three blessings you can count(Things completely out of your control that went your way):

1. _____

2. _____

3. _____

FREE WRITE:

_____

_____

_____

_____

_____

_____

_____

_____

_____

_____

_____

_____

_____

_____

_____

_____

_____

_____

_____

_____

_____

_____

_____

_____

_____

_____

_____

_____

_____

_____

_____

_____

_____

_____

REMINDER: IF YOU'RE ABLE TO READ THIS, THAT MEANS YOU STILL HAVE A PURPOSE OVER YOUR LIFE AND EVERYTHING WITHIN YOU THAT'S NEEDED TO MANIFEST IT.

WEEK 3 | DAY 3

Today's Self-Crowned Focus: _____

Actions to take:

_____

_____

_____

_____

_____

_____

Nightly Check-In:

Wins(How did you crush it today?):

_____

_____

_____

_____

Lessons Learned(Opportunities for improvement?):

_____

_____

_____

_____

Three blessings you can count(Things completely out of your control that went your way):

1. _____

2. _____

3. _____

FREE WRITE:

_____
_____
_____
_____
_____
_____
_____
_____
_____
_____
_____
_____
_____
_____
_____
_____
_____
_____
_____
_____
_____
_____
_____
_____
_____
_____
_____
_____
_____
_____
_____
_____
_____
_____

REMINDER: IF YOU'RE ABLE TO READ THIS, THAT MEANS YOU STILL HAVE A PURPOSE OVER YOUR LIFE AND EVERYTHING WITHIN YOU THAT'S NEEDED TO MANIFEST IT.

WEEK 3 | DAY 4

Today's Self-Crowned Focus: _____

Actions to take:

_____

_____

_____

_____

_____

_____

Nightly Check-In:

Wins(How did you crush it today?):

_____

_____

_____

_____

Lessons Learned(Opportunities for improvement?):

_____

_____

_____

_____

Three blessings you can count(Things completely out of your control that went your way):

1. _____

2. _____

3. _____

FREE WRITE:

_____
_____
_____
_____
_____
_____
_____
_____
_____
_____
_____
_____
_____
_____
_____
_____
_____
_____
_____
_____
_____
_____
_____
_____
_____
_____
_____
_____
_____
_____
_____
_____
_____

REMINDER: IF YOU'RE ABLE TO READ THIS, THAT MEANS YOU STILL HAVE A PURPOSE OVER YOUR LIFE AND EVERYTHING WITHIN YOU THAT'S NEEDED TO MANIFEST IT.

WEEK 3 | DAY 5

Today's Self-Crowned Focus: _____

Actions to take:

_____
_____
_____
_____
_____
_____

Nightly Check-In:

Wins(How did you crush it today?):

_____
_____
_____
_____

Lessons Learned(Opportunities for improvement?):

_____
_____
_____
_____

Three blessings you can count(Things completely out of your control that went your way):

1. _____

2. _____

3. _____

FREE WRITE:

_____

_____

_____

_____

_____

_____

_____

_____

_____

_____

_____

_____

_____

_____

_____

_____

_____

_____

_____

_____

_____

_____

_____

_____

_____

_____

_____

_____

_____

_____

REMINDER: IF YOU'RE ABLE TO READ THIS, THAT MEANS YOU STILL HAVE A PURPOSE OVER YOUR LIFE AND EVERYTHING WITHIN YOU THAT'S NEEDED TO MANIFEST IT.

WEEK 3 | DAY 6

Today's Self-Crowned Focus: _____

Actions to take:

_____
_____
_____
_____
_____
_____

Nightly Check-In:

Wins(How did you crush it today?):

_____
_____
_____
_____

Lessons Learned(Opportunities for improvement?):

_____
_____
_____
_____

Three blessings you can count(Things completely out of your control that went your way):

1. _____
_____

2. _____
_____

3. _____
_____

FREE WRITE:

_____
_____
_____
_____
_____
_____
_____
_____
_____
_____
_____
_____
_____
_____
_____
_____
_____
_____
_____
_____
_____
_____
_____
_____
_____
_____
_____
_____
_____
_____
_____
_____
_____
_____
_____

REMINDER: IF YOU'RE ABLE TO READ THIS, THAT MEANS YOU STILL HAVE A PURPOSE OVER YOUR LIFE AND EVERYTHING WITHIN YOU THAT'S NEEDED TO MANIFEST IT.

WEEK 3 | DAY 7

Today's Self-Crowned Focus: _____

Actions to take:

_____
_____
_____
_____
_____
_____

Nightly Check-In:

Wins(How did you crush it today?):

_____
_____
_____
_____

Lessons Learned(Opportunities for improvement?):

_____
_____
_____
_____

Three blessings you can count(Things completely out of your control that went your way):

1. _____

2. _____

3. _____

FREE WRITE:

_____
_____
_____
_____
_____
_____
_____
_____
_____
_____
_____
_____
_____
_____
_____
_____
_____
_____
_____
_____
_____
_____
_____
_____
_____
_____
_____
_____
_____
_____
_____
_____
_____
_____

REMINDER: IF YOU'RE ABLE TO READ THIS, THAT MEANS YOU STILL HAVE A PURPOSE OVER YOUR LIFE AND EVERYTHING WITHIN YOU THAT'S NEEDED TO MANIFEST IT.

WEEK 3 SCORE CARD

Focus _____

Actions Taken	SUN	MON	TUES	WED	THURS	FRI	SAT	TOTAL
						SUM TOTAL		

Looking at your totals for the week, does it reflect your absolute best effort to have improved in your focus area? _____

Out of all the actions, which one helped you the most?

_____

What are you most proud of yourself for so far?

_____

_____

_____

Realistically, and with your absolute best effort, what do you believe your total sum total will be next week, and how will you achieve this?

_____

_____

_____

FREE WRITE:

_____

_____

_____

_____

_____

_____

_____

_____

_____

_____

_____

_____

_____

_____

_____

_____

_____

_____

_____

_____

_____

_____

_____

_____

_____

_____

_____

_____

_____

_____

_____

_____

_____

REMINDER: IF YOU'RE ABLE TO READ THIS, THAT MEANS YOU STILL HAVE A PURPOSE OVER YOUR LIFE AND EVERYTHING WITHIN YOU THAT'S NEEDED TO MANIFEST IT.

"These days if you want to stop getting hurt, you'd better learn how to miss people while keeping them out of your life."

Derrick Jaxn

"Leaving someone you love so you can be a better you is a temporary pain, but staying and allowing them to hold you back from your full potential is permanent."

Derrick Jaxn

WEEK 4 | DAY 1

Today's Self-Crowned Focus: _____

Actions to take:

_____
_____
_____
_____
_____
_____

Nightly Check-In:

BRAG A LITTLE. YOU DID THAT!

Wins(How did you crush it today?):

_____
_____
_____
_____

NOTHING WRONG WITH MAKING MISTAKES, BUT LET'S ADDRESS THEM.

Lessons Learned(Opportunities for improvement?):

_____
_____
_____
_____

REMIND YOURSELF HOW THE UNIVERSE IS ON YOUR SIDE.

Three blessings you can count(Things completely out of your control that went your way):

1. _____

2. _____

3. _____

FREE WRITE:

_____

_____

_____

_____

_____

_____

_____

_____

_____

_____

_____

_____

_____

_____

_____

_____

_____

_____

_____

_____

_____

_____

_____

_____

_____

_____

_____

_____

_____

_____

_____

REMINDER: IF YOU'RE ABLE TO READ THIS, THAT MEANS YOU STILL HAVE A PURPOSE OVER YOUR LIFE AND EVERYTHING WITHIN YOU THAT'S NEEDED TO MANIFEST IT.

WEEK 4 | DAY 2

Today's Self-Crowned Focus: _____

Actions to take:

_____

_____

_____

_____

_____

_____

Nightly Check-In:

Wins(How did you crush it today?):

_____

_____

_____

_____

Lessons Learned(Opportunities for improvement?):

_____

_____

_____

_____

Three blessings you can count(Things completely out of your control that went your way):

1. _____

2. _____

3. _____

FREE WRITE:

REMINDER: IF YOU'RE ABLE TO READ THIS, THAT MEANS YOU STILL HAVE A PURPOSE OVER YOUR LIFE AND EVERYTHING WITHIN YOU THAT'S NEEDED TO MANIFEST IT.

WEEK 4 | DAY 3

Today's Self-Crowned Focus: _____

Actions to take:

_____
_____
_____
_____
_____
_____

Nightly Check-In:

Wins(How did you crush it today?):

_____
_____
_____
_____

Lessons Learned(Opportunities for improvement?):

_____
_____
_____
_____

Three blessings you can count(Things completely out of your control that went your way):

1. _____

2. _____

3. _____

FREE WRITE:

_____
_____
_____
_____
_____
_____
_____
_____
_____
_____
_____
_____
_____
_____
_____
_____
_____
_____
_____
_____
_____
_____
_____
_____
_____
_____
_____
_____
_____
_____
_____
_____

REMINDER: IF YOU'RE ABLE TO READ THIS, THAT MEANS YOU STILL HAVE A PURPOSE OVER YOUR LIFE AND EVERYTHING WITHIN YOU THAT'S NEEDED TO MANIFEST IT.

WEEK 4 | DAY 4

Today's Self-Crowned Focus: _____

Actions to take:

_____

_____

_____

_____

_____

_____

Nightly Check-In:

BRAG A LITTLE. YOU DID THAT!

Wins(How did you crush it today?):

_____

_____

_____

_____

NOTHING WRONG WITH MAKING MISTAKES, BUT LET'S ADDRESS THEM.

Lessons Learned(Opportunities for improvement?):

_____

_____

_____

_____

REMIND YOURSELF HOW THE UNIVERSE IS ON YOUR SIDE.

Three blessings you can count(Things completely out of your control that went your way):

1. _____

_____

2. _____

_____

3. _____

_____

FREE WRITE:

_____
_____
_____
_____
_____
_____
_____
_____
_____
_____
_____
_____
_____
_____
_____
_____
_____
_____
_____
_____
_____
_____
_____
_____
_____
_____
_____
_____
_____
_____
_____

REMINDER: IF YOU'RE ABLE TO READ THIS, THAT MEANS YOU STILL HAVE A PURPOSE OVER YOUR LIFE AND EVERYTHING WITHIN YOU THAT'S NEEDED TO MANIFEST IT.

WEEK 4 | DAY 5

Today's Self-Crowned Focus: _____

Actions to take:

_____
_____
_____
_____
_____
_____

Nightly Check-In:

BRAG A LITTLE. YOU DID THAT!

Wins(How did you crush it today?):

_____
_____
_____
_____

NOTHING WRONG WITH MAKING MISTAKES, BUT LET'S ADDRESS THEM.

Lessons Learned(Opportunities for improvement?):

_____
_____
_____
_____

REMIND YOURSELF HOW THE UNIVERSE IS ON YOUR SIDE.

Three blessings you can count(Things completely out of your control that went your way):

1. _____

2. _____

3. _____

FREE WRITE:

_____
_____
_____
_____
_____
_____
_____
_____
_____
_____
_____
_____
_____
_____
_____
_____
_____
_____
_____
_____
_____
_____
_____
_____
_____
_____
_____
_____
_____
_____

REMINDER: IF YOU'RE ABLE TO READ THIS, THAT MEANS YOU STILL HAVE A PURPOSE OVER YOUR LIFE AND EVERYTHING WITHIN YOU THAT'S NEEDED TO MANIFEST IT.

WEEK 4 | DAY 6

Today's Self-Crowned Focus: _____

Actions to take:

_____
_____
_____
_____
_____
_____

Nightly Check-In:

Wins(How did you crush it today?):

_____
_____
_____
_____

Lessons Learned(Opportunities for improvement?):

_____
_____
_____
_____

Three blessings you can count(Things completely out of your control that went your way):

1. _____

2. _____

3. _____

FREE WRITE:

_____

_____

_____

_____

_____

_____

_____

_____

_____

_____

_____

_____

_____

_____

_____

_____

_____

_____

_____

_____

_____

_____

_____

_____

_____

_____

_____

_____

_____

_____

_____

_____

_____

REMINDER: IF YOU'RE ABLE TO READ THIS, THAT MEANS YOU STILL HAVE A PURPOSE OVER YOUR LIFE AND EVERYTHING WITHIN YOU THAT'S NEEDED TO MANIFEST IT.

WEEK 4 | DAY 7

Today's Self-Crowned Focus: _____

Actions to take:

_____

_____

_____

_____

_____

_____

Nightly Check-In:

BRAG A LITTLE. YOU DID THAT!

Wins(How did you crush it today?):

_____

_____

_____

_____

NOTHING WRONG WITH MAKING MISTAKES, BUT LET'S ADDRESS THEM.

Lessons Learned(Opportunities for improvement?):

_____

_____

_____

_____

REMIND YOURSELF HOW THE UNIVERSE IS ON YOUR SIDE.

Three blessings you can count(Things completely out of your control that went your way):

1. _____

_____

2. _____

_____

3. _____

_____

FREE WRITE:

_____
_____
_____
_____
_____
_____
_____
_____
_____
_____
_____
_____
_____
_____
_____
_____
_____
_____
_____
_____
_____
_____
_____
_____
_____
_____
_____
_____
_____
_____
_____
_____

REMINDER: IF YOU'RE ABLE TO READ THIS, THAT MEANS YOU STILL HAVE A PURPOSE OVER YOUR LIFE AND EVERYTHING WITHIN YOU THAT'S NEEDED TO MANIFEST IT.

WEEK 4 SCORE CARD

Focus _____

Actions Taken	SUN	MON	TUES	WED	THURS	FRI	SAT	TOTAL
_____								
_____								
_____								
						SUM TOTAL		

Looking at your totals for the week, does it reflect your absolute best effort to have improved in your focus area? _____

Out of all the actions, which one helped you the most?

_____

What are you most proud of yourself for so far?

_____

_____

_____

Realistically, and with your absolute best effort, what do you believe your total sum total will be next week, and how will you achieve this?

_____

_____

_____

FREE WRITE:

_____
_____
_____
_____
_____
_____
_____
_____
_____
_____
_____
_____
_____
_____
_____
_____
_____
_____
_____
_____
_____
_____
_____
_____
_____
_____
_____
_____
_____
_____
_____
_____

REMINDER: IF YOU'RE ABLE TO READ THIS, THAT MEANS YOU STILL HAVE A PURPOSE OVER YOUR LIFE AND EVERYTHING WITHIN YOU THAT'S NEEDED TO MANIFEST IT.

"You can't force people to be who they're not, but you can ALWAYS adjust accordingly once they show you who they are."

Derrick Jaxn

"Never shrink yourself to fit inside the hands of someone who didn't deserve to hold you in the first place."

Derrick Jaxn

WEEK 1 | DAY 1

Today's Self-Crowned Focus: _____

Actions to take:

_____
_____
_____
_____
_____
_____

Nightly Check-In:

BRAG A LITTLE. YOU DID THAT!

Wins(How did you crush it today?):

_____
_____
_____
_____

NOTHING WRONG WITH MAKING MISTAKES, BUT LET'S ADDRESS THEM.

Lessons Learned(Opportunities for improvement?):

_____
_____
_____
_____

REMIND YOURSELF HOW THE UNIVERSE IS ON YOUR SIDE.

Three blessings you can count(Things completely out of your control that went your way):

1. _____

2. _____

3. _____

FREE WRITE:

_____

_____

_____

_____

_____

_____

_____

_____

_____

_____

_____

_____

_____

_____

_____

_____

_____

_____

_____

_____

_____

_____

_____

_____

_____

_____

_____

_____

_____

_____

_____

_____

_____

REMINDER: IF YOU'RE ABLE TO READ THIS, THAT MEANS YOU STILL HAVE A PURPOSE OVER YOUR LIFE AND EVERYTHING WITHIN YOU THAT'S NEEDED TO MANIFEST IT.

WEEK 1 | DAY 2

Today's Self-Crowned Focus: _____

Actions to take:

_____
_____
_____
_____
_____
_____

Nightly Check-In:

Wins(How did you crush it today?):

_____
_____
_____
_____

Lessons Learned(Opportunities for improvement?):

_____
_____
_____
_____

Three blessings you can count(Things completely out of your control that went your way):

1. _____

2. _____

3. _____

_____

FREE WRITE:

_____
_____
_____
_____
_____
_____
_____
_____
_____
_____
_____
_____
_____
_____
_____
_____
_____
_____
_____
_____
_____
_____
_____
_____
_____
_____
_____
_____
_____
_____
_____
_____

REMINDER: IF YOU'RE ABLE TO READ THIS, THAT MEANS YOU STILL HAVE A PURPOSE OVER YOUR LIFE AND EVERYTHING WITHIN YOU THAT'S NEEDED TO MANIFEST IT.

WEEK 1 | DAY 3

Today's Self-Crowned Focus: _____

Actions to take:

_____
_____
_____
_____
_____
_____

Nightly Check-In:

Wins(How did you crush it today?):

_____
_____
_____
_____

Lessons Learned(Opportunities for improvement?):

_____
_____
_____
_____

Three blessings you can count(Things completely out of your control that went your way):

1. _____

2. _____

3. _____

FREE WRITE:

_____
_____
_____
_____
_____
_____
_____
_____
_____
_____
_____
_____
_____
_____
_____
_____
_____
_____
_____
_____
_____
_____
_____
_____
_____
_____
_____
_____
_____
_____
_____
_____
_____
_____

REMINDER: IF YOU'RE ABLE TO READ THIS, THAT MEANS YOU STILL HAVE A PURPOSE OVER YOUR LIFE AND EVERYTHING WITHIN YOU THAT'S NEEDED TO MANIFEST IT.

WEEK 1 | DAY 4

Today's Self-Crowned Focus: _____

Actions to take:

_____

_____

_____

_____

_____

_____

Nightly Check-In:

Wins(How did you crush it today?):

_____

_____

_____

_____

Lessons Learned(Opportunities for improvement?):

_____

_____

_____

_____

Three blessings you can count(Things completely out of your control that went your way):

1. _____

2. _____

3. _____

FREE WRITE:

_____
_____
_____
_____
_____
_____
_____
_____
_____
_____
_____
_____
_____
_____
_____
_____
_____
_____
_____
_____
_____
_____
_____
_____
_____
_____
_____
_____
_____
_____
_____
_____
_____

REMINDER: IF YOU'RE ABLE TO READ THIS, THAT MEANS YOU STILL HAVE A PURPOSE OVER YOUR LIFE AND EVERYTHING WITHIN YOU THAT'S NEEDED TO MANIFEST IT.

WEEK 1 | DAY 5

Today's Self-Crowned Focus: _____

Actions to take:

_____
_____
_____
_____
_____
_____

Nightly Check-In:

Wins(How did you crush it today?):

_____
_____
_____
_____

Lessons Learned(Opportunities for improvement?):

_____
_____
_____
_____

Three blessings you can count(Things completely out of your control that went your way):

1. _____

2. _____

3. _____

FREE WRITE:

_____
_____
_____
_____
_____
_____
_____
_____
_____
_____
_____
_____
_____
_____
_____
_____
_____
_____
_____
_____
_____
_____
_____
_____
_____
_____
_____
_____
_____
_____
_____
_____
_____

REMINDER: IF YOU'RE ABLE TO READ THIS, THAT MEANS YOU STILL HAVE A PURPOSE OVER YOUR LIFE AND EVERYTHING WITHIN YOU THAT'S NEEDED TO MANIFEST IT.

WEEK 1 | DAY 6

Today's Self-Crowned Focus: _____

Actions to take:

_____
_____
_____
_____
_____
_____

Nightly Check-In:

Wins(How did you crush it today?):

_____
_____
_____
_____

Lessons Learned(Opportunities for improvement?):

_____
_____
_____
_____

Three blessings you can count(Things completely out of your control that went your way):

1. _____
_____

2. _____
_____

3. _____
_____

FREE WRITE:

_____
_____
_____
_____
_____
_____
_____
_____
_____
_____
_____
_____
_____
_____
_____
_____
_____
_____
_____
_____
_____
_____
_____
_____
_____
_____
_____
_____
_____
_____
_____
_____
_____
_____
_____

REMINDER: IF YOU'RE ABLE TO READ THIS, THAT MEANS YOU STILL HAVE A PURPOSE OVER YOUR LIFE AND EVERYTHING WITHIN YOU THAT'S NEEDED TO MANIFEST IT.

WEEK 1 | DAY 7

Today's Self-Crowned Focus: _____

Actions to take:

_____
_____
_____
_____
_____
_____

Nightly Check-In:

Wins(How did you crush it today?):

_____
_____
_____
_____

Lessons Learned(Opportunities for improvement?):

_____
_____
_____
_____

Three blessings you can count(Things completely out of your control that went your way):

1. _____
_____

2. _____
_____

3. _____
_____

FREE WRITE:

_____

_____

_____

_____

_____

_____

_____

_____

_____

_____

_____

_____

_____

_____

_____

_____

_____

_____

_____

_____

_____

_____

_____

_____

_____

_____

_____

_____

_____

_____

_____

_____

_____

_____

_____

REMINDER: IF YOU'RE ABLE TO READ THIS, THAT MEANS YOU STILL HAVE A PURPOSE OVER YOUR LIFE AND EVERYTHING WITHIN YOU THAT'S NEEDED TO MANIFEST IT.

WEEK 1 SCORE CARD

Focus _____

Actions Taken	SUN	MON	TUES	WED	THURS	FRI	SAT	TOTAL
					SUM TOTAL			

Looking at your totals for the week, does it reflect your absolute best effort to have improved in your focus area? _____

Out of all the actions, which one helped you the most?

_____

What are you most proud of yourself for so far?

_____

_____

_____

Realistically, and with your absolute best effort, what do you believe your total sum total will be next week, and how will you achieve this?

_____

_____

_____

FREE WRITE:

_____
_____
_____
_____
_____
_____
_____
_____
_____
_____
_____
_____
_____
_____
_____
_____
_____
_____
_____
_____
_____
_____
_____
_____
_____
_____
_____
_____
_____
_____
_____
_____
_____
_____

REMINDER: IF YOU'RE ABLE TO READ THIS, THAT MEANS YOU STILL HAVE A PURPOSE OVER YOUR LIFE AND EVERYTHING WITHIN YOU THAT'S NEEDED TO MANIFEST IT.

"Everyone's not meant to understand you. Stop trying to make them."

Derrick Jaxn

"I don't care how many flaws you have. You deserve to have the love you give people reciprocated."

Derrick Jaxn

WEEK 2 | DAY 1

Today's Self-Crowned Focus: _____

Actions to take:

_____
_____
_____
_____
_____
_____

Nightly Check-In:

Wins(How did you crush it today?):

_____
_____
_____
_____

Lessons Learned(Opportunities for improvement?):

_____
_____
_____
_____

Three blessings you can count(Things completely out of your control that went your way):

1. _____

2. _____

3. _____

FREE WRITE:

_____
_____
_____
_____
_____
_____
_____
_____
_____
_____
_____
_____
_____
_____
_____
_____
_____
_____
_____
_____
_____
_____
_____
_____
_____
_____
_____
_____
_____
_____
_____
_____
_____

REMINDER: IF YOU'RE ABLE TO READ THIS, THAT MEANS YOU STILL HAVE A PURPOSE OVER YOUR LIFE AND EVERYTHING WITHIN YOU THAT'S NEEDED TO MANIFEST IT.

WEEK 2 | DAY 2

Today's Self-Crowned Focus: _____

Actions to take:

_____
_____
_____
_____
_____
_____

Nightly Check-In:

Wins(How did you crush it today?):

_____
_____
_____
_____

Lessons Learned(Opportunities for improvement?):

_____
_____
_____
_____

Three blessings you can count(Things completely out of your control that went your way):

1. _____

2. _____

3. _____
_____

FREE WRITE:

_____
_____
_____
_____
_____
_____
_____
_____
_____
_____
_____
_____
_____
_____
_____
_____
_____
_____
_____
_____
_____
_____
_____
_____
_____
_____
_____
_____
_____
_____
_____
_____
_____
_____

REMINDER: IF YOU'RE ABLE TO READ THIS, THAT MEANS YOU STILL HAVE A PURPOSE OVER YOUR LIFE AND EVERYTHING WITHIN YOU THAT'S NEEDED TO MANIFEST IT.

WEEK 2 | DAY 3

Today's Self-Crowned Focus: _____

Actions to take:

_____

_____

_____

_____

_____

_____

Nightly Check-In:

Wins(How did you crush it today?):

_____

_____

_____

_____

Lessons Learned(Opportunities for improvement?):

_____

_____

_____

_____

Three blessings you can count(Things completely out of your control that went your way):

1. _____

2. _____

3. _____

FREE WRITE:

_____
_____
_____
_____
_____
_____
_____
_____
_____
_____
_____
_____
_____
_____
_____
_____
_____
_____
_____
_____
_____
_____
_____
_____
_____
_____
_____
_____
_____
_____
_____
_____

REMINDER: IF YOU'RE ABLE TO READ THIS, THAT MEANS YOU STILL HAVE A PURPOSE OVER YOUR LIFE AND EVERYTHING WITHIN YOU THAT'S NEEDED TO MANIFEST IT.

WEEK 2 | DAY 4

Today's Self-Crowned Focus: _____

Actions to take:

_____
_____
_____
_____
_____
_____

Nightly Check-In:

Wins(How did you crush it today?):

_____
_____
_____
_____

Lessons Learned(Opportunities for improvement?):

_____
_____
_____
_____

Three blessings you can count(Things completely out of your control that went your way):

1. _____

2. _____

3. _____

FREE WRITE:

_____
_____
_____
_____
_____
_____
_____
_____
_____
_____
_____
_____
_____
_____
_____
_____
_____
_____
_____
_____
_____
_____
_____
_____
_____
_____
_____
_____
_____
_____
_____
_____

REMINDER: IF YOU'RE ABLE TO READ THIS, THAT MEANS YOU STILL HAVE A PURPOSE OVER YOUR LIFE AND EVERYTHING WITHIN YOU THAT'S NEEDED TO MANIFEST IT.

WEEK 2 | DAY 5

Today's Self-Crowned Focus: _____

Actions to take:

_____

_____

_____

_____

_____

_____

Nightly Check-In:

Wins(How did you crush it today?):

_____

_____

_____

_____

Lessons Learned(Opportunities for improvement?):

_____

_____

_____

_____

Three blessings you can count(Things completely out of your control that went your way):

1. _____

_____

2. _____

_____

3. _____

_____

FREE WRITE:

_____
_____
_____
_____
_____
_____
_____
_____
_____
_____
_____
_____
_____
_____
_____
_____
_____
_____
_____
_____
_____
_____
_____
_____
_____
_____
_____
_____
_____
_____
_____
_____
_____
_____

REMINDER: IF YOU'RE ABLE TO READ THIS, THAT MEANS YOU STILL HAVE A PURPOSE OVER YOUR LIFE AND EVERYTHING WITHIN YOU THAT'S NEEDED TO MANIFEST IT.

WEEK 2 | DAY 6

Today's Self-Crowned Focus: _____

Actions to take:

_____
_____
_____
_____
_____
_____

Nightly Check-In:

Wins(How did you crush it today?):

_____
_____
_____
_____

Lessons Learned(Opportunities for improvement?):

_____
_____
_____
_____

Three blessings you can count(Things completely out of your control that went your way):

1. _____

2. _____

3. _____

FREE WRITE:

_____

_____

_____

_____

_____

_____

_____

_____

_____

_____

_____

_____

_____

_____

_____

_____

_____

_____

_____

_____

_____

_____

_____

_____

_____

_____

_____

_____

_____

_____

_____

_____

_____

REMINDER: IF YOU'RE ABLE TO READ THIS, THAT MEANS YOU STILL HAVE A PURPOSE OVER YOUR LIFE AND EVERYTHING WITHIN YOU THAT'S NEEDED TO MANIFEST IT.

WEEK 2 | DAY 7

Today's Self-Crowned Focus: _____

Actions to take:

_____
_____
_____
_____
_____
_____

Nightly Check-In:

Wins(How did you crush it today?):

_____
_____
_____
_____

Lessons Learned(Opportunities for improvement?):

_____
_____
_____
_____

Three blessings you can count(Things completely out of your control that went your way):

1. _____

2. _____

3. _____

FREE WRITE:

_____
_____
_____
_____
_____
_____
_____
_____
_____
_____
_____
_____
_____
_____
_____
_____
_____
_____
_____
_____
_____
_____
_____
_____
_____
_____
_____
_____
_____
_____
_____
_____
_____
_____
_____
_____
_____

REMINDER: IF YOU'RE ABLE TO READ THIS, THAT MEANS YOU STILL HAVE A PURPOSE OVER YOUR LIFE AND EVERYTHING WITHIN YOU THAT'S NEEDED TO MANIFEST IT.

WEEK 2 SCORE CARD

Focus _____

Actions Taken

	SUN	MON	TUES	WED	THURS	FRI	SAT	TOTAL
				SUM TOTAL				

Looking at your totals for the week, does it reflect your absolute best effort to have improved in your focus area? _____

Out of all the actions, which one helped you the most?

_____

What are you most proud of yourself for so far?

_____

_____

_____

Realistically, and with your absolute best effort, what do you believe your total sum total will be next week, and how will you achieve this?

_____

_____

_____

FREE WRITE:

_____
_____
_____
_____
_____
_____
_____
_____
_____
_____
_____
_____
_____
_____
_____
_____
_____
_____
_____
_____
_____
_____
_____
_____
_____
_____
_____
_____
_____
_____
_____
_____
_____
_____
_____

_REMINDER: IF YOU'RE ABLE TO READ THIS, THAT MEANS YOU STILL HAVE A PURPOSE
OVER YOUR LIFE AND EVERYTHING WITHIN YOU THAT'S NEEDED TO MANIFEST IT._

"What would your self-esteem be like if you saw yourself through the eyes of those who love you most instead of those who take you for granted?"

Derrick Jaxn

"Sometimes, you must let them be wrong about you. Maybe they'll get it later, but at least you didn't drain yourself trying to fix them."

Derrick Jaxn

WEEK 3 | DAY 1

Today's Self-Crowned Focus: _____

Actions to take:

_____

_____

_____

_____

_____

_____

Nightly Check-In:

Wins(How did you crush it today?):

_____

_____

_____

_____

Lessons Learned(Opportunities for improvement?):

_____

_____

_____

_____

Three blessings you can count(Things completely out of your control that went your way):

1. _____

2. _____

3. _____

_____

FREE WRITE:

_____
_____
_____
_____
_____
_____
_____
_____
_____
_____
_____
_____
_____
_____
_____
_____
_____
_____
_____
_____
_____
_____
_____
_____
_____
_____
_____
_____
_____
_____

REMINDER: IF YOU'RE ABLE TO READ THIS, THAT MEANS YOU STILL HAVE A PURPOSE OVER YOUR LIFE AND EVERYTHING WITHIN YOU THAT'S NEEDED TO MANIFEST IT.

WEEK 3 | DAY 2

Today's Self-Crowned Focus: _____

Actions to take:

_____

_____

_____

_____

_____

_____

Nightly Check-In:

Wins(How did you crush it today?):

_____

_____

_____

_____

Lessons Learned(Opportunities for improvement?):

_____

_____

_____

_____

Three blessings you can count(Things completely out of your control that went your way):

1. _____

2. _____

3. _____

FREE WRITE:

_____
_____
_____
_____
_____
_____
_____
_____
_____
_____
_____
_____
_____
_____
_____
_____
_____
_____
_____
_____
_____
_____
_____
_____
_____
_____
_____
_____
_____
_____
_____
_____

REMINDER: IF YOU'RE ABLE TO READ THIS, THAT MEANS YOU STILL HAVE A PURPOSE OVER YOUR LIFE AND EVERYTHING WITHIN YOU THAT'S NEEDED TO MANIFEST IT.

WEEK 3 | DAY 3

Today's Self-Crowned Focus: _____

Actions to take:

_____
_____
_____
_____
_____
_____

Nightly Check-In:

Wins(How did you crush it today?):

_____
_____
_____
_____

Lessons Learned(Opportunities for improvement?):

_____
_____
_____
_____

Three blessings you can count(Things completely out of your control that went your way):

1. _____

2. _____

3. _____

FREE WRITE:

_____
_____
_____
_____
_____
_____
_____
_____
_____
_____
_____
_____
_____
_____
_____
_____
_____
_____
_____
_____
_____
_____
_____
_____
_____
_____
_____
_____
_____
_____
_____
_____
_____

REMINDER: IF YOU'RE ABLE TO READ THIS, THAT MEANS YOU STILL HAVE A PURPOSE OVER YOUR LIFE AND EVERYTHING WITHIN YOU THAT'S NEEDED TO MANIFEST IT.

WEEK 3 | DAY 4

Today's Self-Crowned Focus: _____

Actions to take:

_____
_____
_____
_____
_____
_____

Nightly Check-In:

BRAG A LITTLE. YOU DID THAT!

Wins(How did you crush it today?):

_____
_____
_____
_____

NOTHING WRONG WITH MAKING MISTAKES, BUT LET'S ADDRESS THEM.

Lessons Learned(Opportunities for improvement?):

_____
_____
_____
_____

REMIND YOURSELF HOW THE UNIVERSE IS ON YOUR SIDE.

Three blessings you can count(Things completely out of your control that went your way):

1. _____

2. _____

3. _____

FREE WRITE:

_____
_____
_____
_____
_____
_____
_____
_____
_____
_____
_____
_____
_____
_____
_____
_____
_____
_____
_____
_____
_____
_____
_____
_____
_____
_____
_____
_____
_____
_____
_____

REMINDER: IF YOU'RE ABLE TO READ THIS, THAT MEANS YOU STILL HAVE A PURPOSE
OVER YOUR LIFE AND EVERYTHING WITHIN YOU THAT'S NEEDED TO MANIFEST IT.

WEEK 3 | DAY 5

Today's Self-Crowned Focus: _____

Actions to take:

_____

_____

_____

_____

_____

_____

Nightly Check-In:

Wins(How did you crush it today?):

_____

_____

_____

_____

Lessons Learned(Opportunities for improvement?):

_____

_____

_____

_____

Three blessings you can count(Things completely out of your control that went your way):

1. _____

2. _____

3. _____

FREE WRITE:

_____
_____
_____
_____
_____
_____
_____
_____
_____
_____
_____
_____
_____
_____
_____
_____
_____
_____
_____
_____
_____
_____
_____
_____
_____
_____
_____
_____
_____
_____
_____
_____

REMINDER: IF YOU'RE ABLE TO READ THIS, THAT MEANS YOU STILL HAVE A PURPOSE OVER YOUR LIFE AND EVERYTHING WITHIN YOU THAT'S NEEDED TO MANIFEST IT.

WEEK 3 | DAY 6

Today's Self-Crowned Focus: _____

Actions to take:

_____
_____
_____
_____
_____
_____

Nightly Check-In:

Wins(How did you crush it today?):

_____
_____
_____
_____

Lessons Learned(Opportunities for improvement?):

_____
_____
_____
_____

Three blessings you can count(Things completely out of your control that went your way):

1. _____

2. _____

3. _____

FREE WRITE:

_____

_____

_____

_____

_____

_____

_____

_____

_____

_____

_____

_____

_____

_____

_____

_____

_____

_____

_____

_____

_____

_____

_____

_____

_____

_____

_____

_____

_____

_____

_____

_____

_____

REMINDER: IF YOU'RE ABLE TO READ THIS, THAT MEANS YOU STILL HAVE A PURPOSE OVER YOUR LIFE AND EVERYTHING WITHIN YOU THAT'S NEEDED TO MANIFEST IT.

WEEK 3 | DAY 7

Today's Self-Crowned Focus: _____

Actions to take:

_____

_____

_____

_____

_____

_____

Nightly Check-In:

Wins(How did you crush it today?):

_____

_____

_____

_____

Lessons Learned(Opportunities for improvement?):

_____

_____

_____

_____

Three blessings you can count(Things completely out of your control that went your way):

1. _____

_____

2. _____

_____

3. _____

_____

FREE WRITE:

_____
_____
_____
_____
_____
_____
_____
_____
_____
_____
_____
_____
_____
_____
_____
_____
_____
_____
_____
_____
_____
_____
_____
_____
_____
_____
_____
_____
_____
_____
_____
_____

REMINDER: IF YOU'RE ABLE TO READ THIS, THAT MEANS YOU STILL HAVE A PURPOSE OVER YOUR LIFE AND EVERYTHING WITHIN YOU THAT'S NEEDED TO MANIFEST IT.

WEEK 3 SCORE CARD

Focus _____

Actions Taken	SUN	MON	TUES	WED	THURS	FRI	SAT	TOTAL
						SUM TOTAL		

Looking at your totals for the week, does it reflect your absolute best effort to have improved in your focus area? _____

Out of all the actions, which one helped you the most?

_____

What are you most proud of yourself for so far?

_____

_____

_____

Realistically, and with your absolute best effort, what do you believe your total sum total will be next week, and how will you achieve this?

_____

_____

_____

FREE WRITE:

_____
_____
_____
_____
_____
_____
_____
_____
_____
_____
_____
_____
_____
_____
_____
_____
_____
_____
_____
_____
_____
_____
_____
_____
_____
_____
_____
_____
_____
_____
_____

REMINDER: IF YOU'RE ABLE TO READ THIS, THAT MEANS YOU STILL HAVE A PURPOSE OVER YOUR LIFE AND EVERYTHING WITHIN YOU THAT'S NEEDED TO MANIFEST IT.

"Sometimes you gotta put aside what you feel for them and pay attention to what their actions are saying they feel for you."

Derrick Jaxn

"People will call you fake because you stopped putting up with their BS as it being real meant being their doormat."

Derrick Jaxn

WEEK 4 | DAY 1

Today's Self-Crowned Focus: _____

Actions to take:

_____

_____

_____

_____

_____

_____

Nightly Check-In:

Wins(How did you crush it today?):

_____

_____

_____

_____

Lessons Learned(Opportunities for improvement?):

_____

_____

_____

_____

Three blessings you can count(Things completely out of your control that went your way):

1. _____

_____

2. _____

_____

3. _____

_____

FREE WRITE:

_____
_____
_____
_____
_____
_____
_____
_____
_____
_____
_____
_____
_____
_____
_____
_____
_____
_____
_____
_____
_____
_____
_____
_____
_____
_____
_____
_____
_____
_____

REMINDER: IF YOU'RE ABLE TO READ THIS, THAT MEANS YOU STILL HAVE A PURPOSE OVER YOUR LIFE AND EVERYTHING WITHIN YOU THAT'S NEEDED TO MANIFEST IT.

WEEK 4 | DAY 2

Today's Self-Crowned Focus: _____

Actions to take:

_____
_____
_____
_____
_____
_____

Nightly Check-In:

Wins(How did you crush it today?):

_____
_____
_____
_____

Lessons Learned(Opportunities for improvement?):

_____
_____
_____
_____

Three blessings you can count(Things completely out of your control that went your way):

1. _____

2. _____

3. _____

FREE WRITE:

_____
_____
_____
_____
_____
_____
_____
_____
_____
_____
_____
_____
_____
_____
_____
_____
_____
_____
_____
_____
_____
_____
_____
_____
_____
_____
_____
_____
_____
_____
_____
_____
_____
_____
_____

REMINDER: IF YOU'RE ABLE TO READ THIS, THAT MEANS YOU STILL HAVE A PURPOSE OVER YOUR LIFE AND EVERYTHING WITHIN YOU THAT'S NEEDED TO MANIFEST IT.

WEEK 4 | DAY 3

Today's Self-Crowned Focus: _____

Actions to take:

_____
_____
_____
_____
_____
_____

Nightly Check-In:

Wins(How did you crush it today?):

_____
_____
_____
_____

Lessons Learned(Opportunities for improvement?):

_____
_____
_____
_____

Three blessings you can count(Things completely out of your control that went your way):

1. _____

2. _____

3. _____

FREE WRITE:

_____
_____
_____
_____
_____
_____
_____
_____
_____
_____
_____
_____
_____
_____
_____
_____
_____
_____
_____
_____
_____
_____
_____
_____
_____
_____
_____
_____
_____
_____
_____
_____
_____
_____

REMINDER: IF YOU'RE ABLE TO READ THIS, THAT MEANS YOU STILL HAVE A PURPOSE OVER YOUR LIFE AND EVERYTHING WITHIN YOU THAT'S NEEDED TO MANIFEST IT.

WEEK 4 | DAY 4

Today's Self-Crowned Focus: _____

Actions to take:

_____
_____
_____
_____
_____
_____

Nightly Check-In:

Wins(How did you crush it today?):

_____
_____
_____
_____

Lessons Learned(Opportunities for improvement?):

_____
_____
_____
_____

Three blessings you can count(Things completely out of your control that went your way):

1. _____

2. _____

3. _____

FREE WRITE:

_____
_____
_____
_____
_____
_____
_____
_____
_____
_____
_____
_____
_____
_____
_____
_____
_____
_____
_____
_____
_____
_____
_____
_____
_____
_____
_____
_____
_____
_____

REMINDER: IF YOU'RE ABLE TO READ THIS, THAT MEANS YOU STILL HAVE A PURPOSE OVER YOUR LIFE AND EVERYTHING WITHIN YOU THAT'S NEEDED TO MANIFEST IT.

WEEK 4 | DAY 5

Today's Self-Crowned Focus: _____

Actions to take:

_____

_____

_____

_____

_____

_____

Nightly Check-In:

BRAG A LITTLE. YOU DID THAT!

Wins(How did you crush it today?):

_____

_____

_____

_____

NOTHING WRONG WITH MAKING MISTAKES, BUT LET'S ADDRESS THEM.

Lessons Learned(Opportunities for improvement?):

_____

_____

_____

_____

REMIND YOURSELF HOW THE UNIVERSE IS ON YOUR SIDE.

Three blessings you can count(Things completely out of your control that went your way):

1. _____

2. _____

3. _____

FREE WRITE:

_____
_____
_____
_____
_____
_____
_____
_____
_____
_____
_____
_____
_____
_____
_____
_____
_____
_____
_____
_____
_____
_____
_____
_____
_____
_____
_____
_____
_____
_____
_____
_____

REMINDER: IF YOU'RE ABLE TO READ THIS, THAT MEANS YOU STILL HAVE A PURPOSE OVER YOUR LIFE AND EVERYTHING WITHIN YOU THAT'S NEEDED TO MANIFEST IT.

WEEK 4 | DAY 6

Today's Self-Crowned Focus: _____

Actions to take:

_____
_____
_____
_____
_____
_____

Nightly Check-In:

Wins(How did you crush it today?):

_____
_____
_____
_____

Lessons Learned(Opportunities for improvement?):

_____
_____
_____
_____

Three blessings you can count(Things completely out of your control that went your way):

1. _____

2. _____

3. _____
_____

FREE WRITE:

_____
_____
_____
_____
_____
_____
_____
_____
_____
_____
_____
_____
_____
_____
_____
_____
_____
_____
_____
_____
_____
_____
_____
_____
_____
_____
_____
_____
_____
_____
_____
_____
_____
_____

REMINDER: IF YOU'RE ABLE TO READ THIS, THAT MEANS YOU STILL HAVE A PURPOSE OVER YOUR LIFE AND EVERYTHING WITHIN YOU THAT'S NEEDED TO MANIFEST IT.

WEEK 4 | DAY 7

Today's Self-Crowned Focus: _____

Actions to take:

_____

_____

_____

_____

_____

_____

Nightly Check-In:

Wins(How did you crush it today?):

_____

_____

_____

_____

Lessons Learned(Opportunities for improvement?):

_____

_____

_____

_____

Three blessings you can count(Things completely out of your control that went your way):

1. _____

2. _____

3. _____

FREE WRITE:

_____
_____
_____
_____
_____
_____
_____
_____
_____
_____
_____
_____
_____
_____
_____
_____
_____
_____
_____
_____
_____
_____
_____
_____
_____
_____
_____
_____
_____
_____
_____
_____
_____
_____
_____

REMINDER: IF YOU'RE ABLE TO READ THIS, THAT MEANS YOU STILL HAVE A PURPOSE OVER YOUR LIFE AND EVERYTHING WITHIN YOU THAT'S NEEDED TO MANIFEST IT.

WEEK 4 SCORE CARD

Focus _____

Actions Taken

	SUN	MON	TUES	WED	THURS	FRI	SAT	TOTAL
						SUM TOTAL		

Looking at your totals for the week, does it reflect your absolute best effort to have improved in your focus area? _____

Out of all the actions, which one helped you the most?

_____

What are you most proud of yourself for so far?

_____

_____

_____

Realistically, and with your absolute best effort, what do you believe your total sum total will be next week, and how will you achieve this?

_____

_____

_____

FREE WRITE:

_____
_____
_____
_____
_____
_____
_____
_____
_____
_____
_____
_____
_____
_____
_____
_____
_____
_____
_____
_____
_____
_____
_____
_____
_____
_____
_____
_____
_____
_____
_____
_____

REMINDER: IF YOU'RE ABLE TO READ THIS, THAT MEANS YOU STILL HAVE A PURPOSE OVER YOUR LIFE AND EVERYTHING WITHIN YOU THAT'S NEEDED TO MANIFEST IT.

"It doesn't matter how much, how hard, or how deeply you love someone. If they don't know how to receive it, it will be rejected."

Derrick Jaxn

"You can't be loyal to your growth while remaining loyal to someone who isn't growing. You'll eventually have to choose one."

Derrick Jaxn

WEEK 1 | DAY 1

Today's Self-Crowned Focus: _____

Actions to take:

_____

_____

_____

_____

_____

_____

Nightly Check-In:

Wins(How did you crush it today?):

_____

_____

_____

_____

Lessons Learned(Opportunities for improvement?):

_____

_____

_____

_____

Three blessings you can count(Things completely out of your control that went your way):

1. _____

2. _____

3. _____

FREE WRITE:

_____
_____
_____
_____
_____
_____
_____
_____
_____
_____
_____
_____
_____
_____
_____
_____
_____
_____
_____
_____
_____
_____
_____
_____
_____
_____
_____
_____
_____
_____
_____
_____

REMINDER: IF YOU'RE ABLE TO READ THIS, THAT MEANS YOU STILL HAVE A PURPOSE OVER YOUR LIFE AND EVERYTHING WITHIN YOU THAT'S NEEDED TO MANIFEST IT.

WEEK 1 | DAY 2

Today's Self-Crowned Focus: _____

Actions to take:

_____
_____
_____
_____
_____
_____

Nightly Check-In:

Wins(How did you crush it today?):

_____
_____
_____
_____

Lessons Learned(Opportunities for improvement?):

_____
_____
_____
_____

Three blessings you can count(Things completely out of your control that went your way):

1. _____

2. _____

3. _____
_____

FREE WRITE:

_____

_____

_____

_____

_____

_____

_____

_____

_____

_____

_____

_____

_____

_____

_____

_____

_____

_____

_____

_____

_____

_____

_____

_____

_____

_____

_____

_____

_____

_____

_____

_____

_____

_____

REMINDER: IF YOU'RE ABLE TO READ THIS, THAT MEANS YOU STILL HAVE A PURPOSE OVER YOUR LIFE AND EVERYTHING WITHIN YOU THAT'S NEEDED TO MANIFEST IT.

WEEK 1 | DAY 3

Today's Self-Crowned Focus: _____

Actions to take:

_____

_____

_____

_____

_____

_____

Nightly Check-In:

Wins(How did you crush it today?):

_____

_____

_____

_____

Lessons Learned(Opportunities for improvement?):

_____

_____

_____

_____

Three blessings you can count(Things completely out of your control that went your way):

1. _____

2. _____

3. _____

_____

FREE WRITE:

_____
_____
_____
_____
_____
_____
_____
_____
_____
_____
_____
_____
_____
_____
_____
_____
_____
_____
_____
_____
_____
_____
_____
_____
_____
_____
_____
_____
_____
_____
_____
_____
_____

REMINDER: IF YOU'RE ABLE TO READ THIS, THAT MEANS YOU STILL HAVE A PURPOSE OVER YOUR LIFE AND EVERYTHING WITHIN YOU THAT'S NEEDED TO MANIFEST IT.

WEEK 1 | DAY 4

Today's Self-Crowned Focus: _____

Actions to take:

_____
_____
_____
_____
_____
_____

Nightly Check-In:

Wins(How did you crush it today?):

_____
_____
_____
_____

Lessons Learned(Opportunities for improvement?):

_____
_____
_____
_____

Three blessings you can count(Things completely out of your control that went your way):

1. _____

2. _____

3. _____

FREE WRITE:

_____
_____
_____
_____
_____
_____
_____
_____
_____
_____
_____
_____
_____
_____
_____
_____
_____
_____
_____
_____
_____
_____
_____
_____
_____
_____
_____
_____
_____
_____
_____
_____
_____

REMINDER: IF YOU'RE ABLE TO READ THIS, THAT MEANS YOU STILL HAVE A PURPOSE OVER YOUR LIFE AND EVERYTHING WITHIN YOU THAT'S NEEDED TO MANIFEST IT.

WEEK 1 | DAY 5

Today's Self-Crowned Focus: _____

Actions to take:

_____
_____
_____
_____
_____
_____

Nightly Check-In:

Wins(How did you crush it today?):

_____
_____
_____
_____

Lessons Learned(Opportunities for improvement?):

_____
_____
_____
_____

Three blessings you can count(Things completely out of your control that went your way):

1. _____

2. _____

3. _____

FREE WRITE:

_____
_____
_____
_____
_____
_____
_____
_____
_____
_____
_____
_____
_____
_____
_____
_____
_____
_____
_____
_____
_____
_____
_____
_____
_____
_____
_____
_____
_____
_____
_____

REMINDER: IF YOU'RE ABLE TO READ THIS, THAT MEANS YOU STILL HAVE A PURPOSE OVER YOUR LIFE AND EVERYTHING WITHIN YOU THAT'S NEEDED TO MANIFEST IT.

WEEK 1 | DAY 6

Today's Self-Crowned Focus: _____

Actions to take:

_____
_____
_____
_____
_____
_____

Nightly Check-In:

Wins(How did you crush it today?):

_____
_____
_____
_____

Lessons Learned(Opportunities for improvement?):

_____
_____
_____
_____

Three blessings you can count(Things completely out of your control that went your way):

1. _____

2. _____

3. _____

FREE WRITE:

_____
_____
_____
_____
_____
_____
_____
_____
_____
_____
_____
_____
_____
_____
_____
_____
_____
_____
_____
_____
_____
_____
_____
_____
_____
_____
_____
_____
_____
_____
_____
_____
_____
_____

REMINDER: IF YOU'RE ABLE TO READ THIS, THAT MEANS YOU STILL HAVE A PURPOSE OVER YOUR LIFE AND EVERYTHING WITHIN YOU THAT'S NEEDED TO MANIFEST IT.

WEEK 1 | DAY 7

Today's Self-Crowned Focus: _____

Actions to take:

_____
_____
_____
_____
_____
_____

Nightly Check-In:

Wins(How did you crush it today?):

_____
_____
_____
_____

Lessons Learned(Opportunities for improvement?):

_____
_____
_____
_____

Three blessings you can count(Things completely out of your control that went your way):

1. _____

2. _____

3. _____

FREE WRITE:

_____

_____

_____

_____

_____

_____

_____

_____

_____

_____

_____

_____

_____

_____

_____

_____

_____

_____

_____

_____

_____

_____

_____

_____

_____

_____

_____

_____

_____

_____

_____

_____

_____

_____

REMINDER: IF YOU'RE ABLE TO READ THIS, THAT MEANS YOU STILL HAVE A PURPOSE OVER YOUR LIFE AND EVERYTHING WITHIN YOU THAT'S NEEDED TO MANIFEST IT.

WEEK 1 SCORE CARD

Focus _____

Actions Taken

	SUN	MON	TUES	WED	THURS	FRI	SAT	TOTAL
							SUM TOTAL	

Looking at your totals for the week, does it reflect your absolute best effort to have improved in your focus area? _____

Out of all the actions, which one helped you the most?

_____

What are you most proud of yourself for so far?

_____

_____

_____

Realistically, and with your absolute best effort, what do you believe your total sum total will be next week, and how will you achieve this?

_____

_____

_____

FREE WRITE:

_____
_____
_____
_____
_____
_____
_____
_____
_____
_____
_____
_____
_____
_____
_____
_____
_____
_____
_____
_____
_____
_____
_____
_____
_____
_____
_____
_____
_____

_REMINDER: IF YOU'RE ABLE TO READ THIS, THAT MEANS YOU STILL HAVE A PURPOSE
OVER YOUR LIFE AND EVERYTHING WITHIN YOU THAT'S NEEDED TO MANIFEST IT._

"Never settle for someone who's only loving you part-time. Your worth goes beyond what minimum-wage effort can afford!"

Derrick Jaxn

"You can't be loyal to your growth while remaining loyal to someone who isn't growing. You'll eventually have to choose one."

Derrick Jaxn

FREE WRITE:

_____
_____
_____
_____
_____
_____
_____
_____
_____
_____
_____
_____
_____
_____
_____
_____
_____
_____
_____
_____
_____
_____
_____
_____
_____
_____
_____
_____
_____
_____

REMINDER: IF YOU'RE ABLE TO READ THIS, THAT MEANS YOU STILL HAVE A PURPOSE OVER YOUR LIFE AND EVERYTHING WITHIN YOU THAT'S NEEDED TO MANIFEST IT.

WEEK 2 | DAY 2

Today's Self-Crowned Focus: _____

Actions to take:

_____
_____
_____
_____
_____
_____

Nightly Check-In:

Wins(How did you crush it today?):

_____
_____
_____
_____

Lessons Learned(Opportunities for improvement?):

_____
_____
_____
_____

Three blessings you can count(Things completely out of your control that went your way):

1. _____

2. _____

3. _____

FREE WRITE:

_____

_____

_____

_____

_____

_____

_____

_____

_____

_____

_____

_____

_____

_____

_____

_____

_____

_____

_____

_____

_____

_____

_____

_____

_____

_____

_____

_____

_____

_____

_____

_____

_____

_____

_____

REMINDER: IF YOU'RE ABLE TO READ THIS, THAT MEANS YOU STILL HAVE A PURPOSE OVER YOUR LIFE AND EVERYTHING WITHIN YOU THAT'S NEEDED TO MANIFEST IT.

WEEK 2 | DAY 3

Today's Self-Crowned Focus: _____

Actions to take:

_____
_____
_____
_____
_____
_____

Nightly Check-In:

Wins(How did you crush it today?):

_____
_____
_____
_____

Lessons Learned(Opportunities for improvement?):

_____
_____
_____
_____

Three blessings you can count(Things completely out of your control that went your way):

1. _____

2. _____

3. _____

FREE WRITE:

_____
_____
_____
_____
_____
_____
_____
_____
_____
_____
_____
_____
_____
_____
_____
_____
_____
_____
_____
_____
_____
_____
_____
_____
_____
_____
_____
_____
_____
_____
_____
_____

REMINDER: IF YOU'RE ABLE TO READ THIS, THAT MEANS YOU STILL HAVE A PURPOSE OVER YOUR LIFE AND EVERYTHING WITHIN YOU THAT'S NEEDED TO MANIFEST IT.

WEEK 2 | DAY 4

Today's Self-Crowned Focus: _____

Actions to take:

_____
_____
_____
_____
_____
_____

Nightly Check-In:

Wins(How did you crush it today?):

_____
_____
_____
_____

Lessons Learned(Opportunities for improvement?):

_____
_____
_____
_____

Three blessings you can count(Things completely out of your control that went your way):

1. _____

2. _____

3. _____

FREE WRITE:

_____

_____

_____

_____

_____

_____

_____

_____

_____

_____

_____

_____

_____

_____

_____

_____

_____

_____

_____

_____

_____

_____

_____

_____

_____

_____

_____

_____

_____

_____

_____

_____

_____

_____

_____

REMINDER: IF YOU'RE ABLE TO READ THIS, THAT MEANS YOU STILL HAVE A PURPOSE OVER YOUR LIFE AND EVERYTHING WITHIN YOU THAT'S NEEDED TO MANIFEST IT.

WEEK 2 | DAY 5

Today's Self-Crowned Focus: _____

Actions to take:

_____

_____

_____

_____

_____

_____

Nightly Check-In:

Wins(How did you crush it today?):

_____

_____

_____

_____

Lessons Learned(Opportunities for improvement?):

_____

_____

_____

_____

Three blessings you can count(Things completely out of your control that went your way):

1. _____

2. _____

3. _____

FREE WRITE:

_____
_____
_____
_____
_____
_____
_____
_____
_____
_____
_____
_____
_____
_____
_____
_____
_____
_____
_____
_____
_____
_____
_____
_____
_____
_____
_____
_____
_____
_____
_____

REMINDER: IF YOU'RE ABLE TO READ THIS, THAT MEANS YOU STILL HAVE A PURPOSE OVER YOUR LIFE AND EVERYTHING WITHIN YOU THAT'S NEEDED TO MANIFEST IT.

WEEK 2 | DAY 6

Today's Self-Crowned Focus: _____

Actions to take:

_____
_____
_____
_____
_____
_____

Nightly Check-In:

Wins(How did you crush it today?):

_____
_____
_____
_____

Lessons Learned(Opportunities for improvement?):

_____
_____
_____
_____

Three blessings you can count(Things completely out of your control that went your way):

1. _____

2. _____

3. _____

FREE WRITE:

_____
_____
_____
_____
_____
_____
_____
_____
_____
_____
_____
_____
_____
_____
_____
_____
_____
_____
_____
_____
_____
_____
_____
_____
_____
_____
_____
_____
_____
_____
_____
_____
_____
_____

REMINDER: IF YOU'RE ABLE TO READ THIS, THAT MEANS YOU STILL HAVE A PURPOSE OVER YOUR LIFE AND EVERYTHING WITHIN YOU THAT'S NEEDED TO MANIFEST IT.

WEEK 2 | DAY 7

Today's Self-Crowned Focus: _____

Actions to take:

_____
_____
_____
_____
_____
_____

Nightly Check-In:

Wins(How did you crush it today?):

_____
_____
_____
_____

Lessons Learned(Opportunities for improvement?):

_____
_____
_____
_____

Three blessings you can count(Things completely out of your control that went your way):

1. _____
_____

2. _____
_____

3. _____
_____

FREE WRITE:

REMINDER: IF YOU'RE ABLE TO READ THIS, THAT MEANS YOU STILL HAVE A PURPOSE OVER YOUR LIFE AND EVERYTHING WITHIN YOU THAT'S NEEDED TO MANIFEST IT.

WEEK 2 SCORE CARD

Focus _____

Actions Taken	SUN	MON	TUES	WED	THURS	FRI	SAT	TOTAL
						SUM TOTAL		

Looking at your totals for the week, does it reflect your absolute best effort to have improved in your focus area? _____

Out of all the actions, which one helped you the most?

_____

What are you most proud of yourself for so far?

_____

_____

_____

Realistically, and with your absolute best effort, what do you believe your total sum total will be next week, and how will you achieve this?

_____

_____

_____

FREE WRITE:

_____
_____
_____
_____
_____
_____
_____
_____
_____
_____
_____
_____
_____
_____
_____
_____
_____
_____
_____
_____
_____
_____
_____
_____
_____
_____
_____
_____
_____
_____

REMINDER: IF YOU'RE ABLE TO READ THIS, THAT MEANS YOU STILL HAVE A PURPOSE OVER YOUR LIFE AND EVERYTHING WITHIN YOU THAT'S NEEDED TO MANIFEST IT.

"Never let someone convince you that holding them accountable for their actions is you creating negativity, stress, or drama. If they didn't want the task of loving you correctly, they should've never signed up for it."

Derrick Jaxn

"Stop waiting and wishing for a position in anyone's life. You don't have to stand in line for a seat that already has your name on it."

Derrick Jaxn

WEEK 3 | DAY 1

Today's Self-Crowned Focus: _____

Actions to take:

_____
_____
_____
_____
_____
_____

Nightly Check-In:

Wins(How did you crush it today?):

_____
_____
_____
_____

Lessons Learned(Opportunities for improvement?):

_____
_____
_____
_____

Three blessings you can count(Things completely out of your control that went your way):

1. _____
_____

2. _____
_____

3. _____
_____

FREE WRITE:

_____
_____
_____
_____
_____
_____
_____
_____
_____
_____
_____
_____
_____
_____
_____
_____
_____
_____
_____
_____
_____
_____
_____
_____
_____
_____
_____
_____
_____
_____
_____
_____
_____
_____
_____

REMINDER: IF YOU'RE ABLE TO READ THIS, THAT MEANS YOU STILL HAVE A PURPOSE OVER YOUR LIFE AND EVERYTHING WITHIN YOU THAT'S NEEDED TO MANIFEST IT.

WEEK 3 | DAY 2

Today's Self-Crowned Focus: _____

Actions to take:

_____
_____
_____
_____
_____
_____

Nightly Check-In:

Wins(How did you crush it today?):

_____
_____
_____
_____

Lessons Learned(Opportunities for improvement?):

_____
_____
_____
_____

Three blessings you can count(Things completely out of your control that went your way):

1. _____
_____

2. _____
_____

3. _____
_____

FREE WRITE:

_____
_____
_____
_____
_____
_____
_____
_____
_____
_____
_____
_____
_____
_____
_____
_____
_____
_____
_____
_____
_____
_____
_____
_____
_____
_____
_____
_____
_____
_____
_____
_____

REMINDER: IF YOU'RE ABLE TO READ THIS, THAT MEANS YOU STILL HAVE A PURPOSE OVER YOUR LIFE AND EVERYTHING WITHIN YOU THAT'S NEEDED TO MANIFEST IT.

WEEK 3 | DAY 3

Today's Self-Crowned Focus: _____

Actions to take:

_____

_____

_____

_____

_____

_____

Nightly Check-In:

Wins(How did you crush it today?):

_____

_____

_____

_____

Lessons Learned(Opportunities for improvement?):

_____

_____

_____

_____

Three blessings you can count(Things completely out of your control that went your way):

1. _____

_____

2. _____

_____

3. _____

_____

FREE WRITE:

_____
_____
_____
_____
_____
_____
_____
_____
_____
_____
_____
_____
_____
_____
_____
_____
_____
_____
_____
_____
_____
_____
_____
_____
_____
_____
_____
_____
_____
_____
_____
_____
_____
_____

REMINDER: IF YOU'RE ABLE TO READ THIS, THAT MEANS YOU STILL HAVE A PURPOSE OVER YOUR LIFE AND EVERYTHING WITHIN YOU THAT'S NEEDED TO MANIFEST IT.

WEEK 3 | DAY 4

Today's Self-Crowned Focus: _____

Actions to take:

_____

_____

_____

_____

_____

_____

Nightly Check-In:

Wins(How did you crush it today?):

_____

_____

_____

_____

Lessons Learned(Opportunities for improvement?):

_____

_____

_____

_____

Three blessings you can count(Things completely out of your control that went your way):

1. _____

_____

2. _____

_____

3. _____

_____

FREE WRITE:

_____
_____
_____
_____
_____
_____
_____
_____
_____
_____
_____
_____
_____
_____
_____
_____
_____
_____
_____
_____
_____
_____
_____
_____
_____
_____
_____
_____
_____
_____
_____
_____

REMINDER: IF YOU'RE ABLE TO READ THIS, THAT MEANS YOU STILL HAVE A PURPOSE OVER YOUR LIFE AND EVERYTHING WITHIN YOU THAT'S NEEDED TO MANIFEST IT.

WEEK 3 | DAY 5

Today's Self-Crowned Focus: _____

Actions to take:

_____

_____

_____

_____

_____

_____

Nightly Check-In:

BRAG A LITTLE. YOU DID THAT!

Wins(How did you crush it today?):

_____

_____

_____

_____

NOTHING WRONG WITH MAKING MISTAKES, BUT LET'S ADDRESS THEM.

Lessons Learned(Opportunities for improvement?):

_____

_____

_____

_____

REMIND YOURSELF HOW THE UNIVERSE IS ON YOUR SIDE.

Three blessings you can count(Things completely out of your control that went your way):

1. _____

_____

2. _____

_____

3. _____

_____

FREE WRITE:

REMINDER: IF YOU'RE ABLE TO READ THIS, THAT MEANS YOU STILL HAVE A PURPOSE OVER YOUR LIFE AND EVERYTHING WITHIN YOU THAT'S NEEDED TO MANIFEST IT.

WEEK 3 | DAY 6

Today's Self-Crowned Focus: _____

Actions to take:

_____
_____
_____
_____
_____
_____

Nightly Check-In:

Wins(How did you crush it today?):

_____
_____
_____
_____

Lessons Learned(Opportunities for improvement?):

_____
_____
_____
_____

Three blessings you can count(Things completely out of your control that went your way):

1. _____

2. _____

3. _____

FREE WRITE:

_____
_____
_____
_____
_____
_____
_____
_____
_____
_____
_____
_____
_____
_____
_____
_____
_____
_____
_____
_____
_____
_____
_____
_____
_____
_____
_____
_____
_____
_____
_____

REMINDER: IF YOU'RE ABLE TO READ THIS, THAT MEANS YOU STILL HAVE A PURPOSE OVER YOUR LIFE AND EVERYTHING WITHIN YOU THAT'S NEEDED TO MANIFEST IT.

WEEK 3 | DAY 7

Today's Self-Crowned Focus: _____

Actions to take:

_____
_____
_____
_____
_____
_____

Nightly Check-In:

Wins(How did you crush it today?):

_____
_____
_____
_____

Lessons Learned(Opportunities for improvement?):

_____
_____
_____
_____

Three blessings you can count(Things completely out of your control that went your way):

1. _____
_____

2. _____
_____

3. _____
_____

FREE WRITE:

_____
_____
_____
_____
_____
_____
_____
_____
_____
_____
_____
_____
_____
_____
_____
_____
_____
_____
_____
_____
_____
_____
_____
_____
_____
_____
_____
_____
_____
_____
_____
_____
_____

REMINDER: IF YOU'RE ABLE TO READ THIS, THAT MEANS YOU STILL HAVE A PURPOSE OVER YOUR LIFE AND EVERYTHING WITHIN YOU THAT'S NEEDED TO MANIFEST IT.

WEEK 3 SCORE CARD

Focus _____

Actions Taken	SUN	MON	TUES	WED	THURS	FRI	SAT	TOTAL
						SUM TOTAL		

Looking at your totals for the week, does it reflect your absolute best effort to have improved in your focus area? _____

Out of all the actions, which one helped you the most?

_____

What are you most proud of yourself for so far?

_____

_____

_____

Realistically, and with your absolute best effort, what do you believe your total sum total will be next week, and how will you achieve this?

_____

_____

_____

FREE WRITE:

_____

_____

_____

_____

_____

_____

_____

_____

_____

_____

_____

_____

_____

_____

_____

_____

_____

_____

_____

_____

_____

_____

_____

_____

_____

_____

_____

_____

_____

_____

_____

_____

REMINDER: IF YOU'RE ABLE TO READ THIS, THAT MEANS YOU STILL HAVE A PURPOSE OVER YOUR LIFE AND EVERYTHING WITHIN YOU THAT'S NEEDED TO MANIFEST IT.

"Bigger hearts have more to break because they have more to give which tends to be too much for most."

Derrick Jaxn

"Some men aren't intimidated by a strong woman, they're just turned off by their inability to control her. There's a difference."

Derrick Jaxn

WEEK 4 | DAY 1

Today's Self-Crowned Focus: _____

Actions to take:

_____
_____
_____
_____
_____
_____

Nightly Check-In:

Wins(How did you crush it today?):

_____
_____
_____
_____

Lessons Learned(Opportunities for improvement?):

_____
_____
_____
_____

Three blessings you can count(Things completely out of your control that went your way):

1. _____

2. _____

3. _____

FREE WRITE:

REMINDER: IF YOU'RE ABLE TO READ THIS, THAT MEANS YOU STILL HAVE A PURPOSE OVER YOUR LIFE AND EVERYTHING WITHIN YOU THAT'S NEEDED TO MANIFEST IT.

WEEK 4 | DAY 2

Today's Self-Crowned Focus: _____

Actions to take:

_____
_____
_____
_____
_____
_____

Nightly Check-In:

Wins(How did you crush it today?):

_____
_____
_____
_____

Lessons Learned(Opportunities for improvement?):

_____
_____
_____
_____

Three blessings you can count(Things completely out of your control that went your way):

1. _____
_____

2. _____
_____

3. _____
_____

FREE WRITE:

_____
_____
_____
_____
_____
_____
_____
_____
_____
_____
_____
_____
_____
_____
_____
_____
_____
_____
_____
_____
_____
_____
_____
_____
_____
_____
_____
_____
_____
_____
_____
_____

REMINDER: IF YOU'RE ABLE TO READ THIS, THAT MEANS YOU STILL HAVE A PURPOSE OVER YOUR LIFE AND EVERYTHING WITHIN YOU THAT'S NEEDED TO MANIFEST IT.

WEEK 4 | DAY 3

Today's Self-Crowned Focus: _____

Actions to take:

_____

_____

_____

_____

_____

_____

Nightly Check-In:

Wins(How did you crush it today?):

_____

_____

_____

_____

Lessons Learned(Opportunities for improvement?):

_____

_____

_____

_____

Three blessings you can count(Things completely out of your control that went your way):

1. _____

2. _____

3. _____

FREE WRITE:

_____
_____
_____
_____
_____
_____
_____
_____
_____
_____
_____
_____
_____
_____
_____
_____
_____
_____
_____
_____
_____
_____
_____
_____
_____
_____
_____
_____
_____
_____
_____

REMINDER: IF YOU'RE ABLE TO READ THIS, THAT MEANS YOU STILL HAVE A PURPOSE OVER YOUR LIFE AND EVERYTHING WITHIN YOU THAT'S NEEDED TO MANIFEST IT.

WEEK 4 | DAY 4

Today's Self-Crowned Focus: _____

Actions to take:

_____

_____

_____

_____

_____

_____

Nightly Check-In:

BRAG A LITTLE. YOU DID THAT!

Wins(How did you crush it today?):

_____

_____

_____

_____

NOTHING WRONG WITH MAKING MISTAKES, BUT LET'S ADDRESS THEM.

Lessons Learned(Opportunities for improvement?):

_____

_____

_____

_____

REMIND YOURSELF HOW THE UNIVERSE IS ON YOUR SIDE.

Three blessings you can count(Things completely out of your control that went your way):

1. _____

_____

2. _____

_____

3. _____

_____

FREE WRITE:

_____
_____
_____
_____
_____
_____
_____
_____
_____
_____
_____
_____
_____
_____
_____
_____
_____
_____
_____
_____
_____
_____
_____
_____
_____
_____
_____
_____
_____
_____
_____
_____
_____

_REMINDER: IF YOU'RE ABLE TO READ THIS, THAT MEANS YOU STILL HAVE A PURPOSE
OVER YOUR LIFE AND EVERYTHING WITHIN YOU THAT'S NEEDED TO MANIFEST IT._

WEEK 4 | DAY 5

Today's Self-Crowned Focus: _____

Actions to take:

_____
_____
_____
_____
_____
_____

Nightly Check-In:

Wins(How did you crush it today?):

_____
_____
_____
_____

Lessons Learned(Opportunities for improvement?):

_____
_____
_____
_____

Three blessings you can count(Things completely out of your control that went your way):

1. _____

2. _____

3. _____

FREE WRITE:

_____
_____
_____
_____
_____
_____
_____
_____
_____
_____
_____
_____
_____
_____
_____
_____
_____
_____
_____
_____
_____
_____
_____
_____
_____
_____
_____
_____
_____
_____
_____

REMINDER: IF YOU'RE ABLE TO READ THIS, THAT MEANS YOU STILL HAVE A PURPOSE OVER YOUR LIFE AND EVERYTHING WITHIN YOU THAT'S NEEDED TO MANIFEST IT.

WEEK 4 | DAY 6

Today's Self-Crowned Focus: _____

Actions to take:

_____
_____
_____
_____
_____
_____

Nightly Check-In:

Wins(How did you crush it today?):

_____
_____
_____
_____

Lessons Learned(Opportunities for improvement?):

_____
_____
_____
_____

Three blessings you can count(Things completely out of your control that went your way):

1. _____
_____

2. _____
_____

3. _____
_____

FREE WRITE:

_____
_____
_____
_____
_____
_____
_____
_____
_____
_____
_____
_____
_____
_____
_____
_____
_____
_____
_____
_____
_____
_____
_____
_____
_____
_____
_____
_____
_____
_____

REMINDER: IF YOU'RE ABLE TO READ THIS, THAT MEANS YOU STILL HAVE A PURPOSE OVER YOUR LIFE AND EVERYTHING WITHIN YOU THAT'S NEEDED TO MANIFEST IT.

WEEK 4 | DAY 7

Today's Self-Crowned Focus: _____

Actions to take:

_____
_____
_____
_____
_____
_____

Nightly Check-In:

Wins(How did you crush it today?):

_____
_____
_____
_____

Lessons Learned(Opportunities for improvement?):

_____
_____
_____
_____

Three blessings you can count(Things completely out of your control that went your way):

1. _____
_____

2. _____
_____

3. _____
_____

FREE WRITE:

_____

_____

_____

_____

_____

_____

_____

_____

_____

_____

_____

_____

_____

_____

_____

_____

_____

_____

_____

_____

_____

_____

_____

_____

_____

_____

_____

_____

_____

_____

REMINDER: IF YOU'RE ABLE TO READ THIS, THAT MEANS YOU STILL HAVE A PURPOSE OVER YOUR LIFE AND EVERYTHING WITHIN YOU THAT'S NEEDED TO MANIFEST IT.

WEEK 4 SCORE CARD

Focus _____

Actions Taken	SUN	MON	TUES	WED	THURS	FRI	SAT	TOTAL
_____								
_____								
_____								
						SUM TOTAL		

Looking at your totals for the week, does it reflect your absolute best effort to have improved in your focus area? _____

Out of all the actions, which one helped you the most?

_____

What are you most proud of yourself for so far?

_____
_____
_____

Realistically, and with your absolute best effort, what do you believe your total sum total will be next week, and how will you achieve this?

_____
_____
_____

FREE WRITE:

_____
_____
_____
_____
_____
_____
_____
_____
_____
_____
_____
_____
_____
_____
_____
_____
_____
_____
_____
_____
_____
_____
_____
_____
_____
_____
_____
_____
_____
_____
_____
_____
_____

REMINDER: IF YOU'RE ABLE TO READ THIS, THAT MEANS YOU STILL HAVE A PURPOSE OVER YOUR LIFE AND EVERYTHING WITHIN YOU THAT'S NEEDED TO MANIFEST IT.

"Make peace with the version of yourself you've outgrown. Let go of those who can't do the same."

Derrick Jaxn

"Self-care is understanding that just because anyone could benefit from having you doesn't mean just anyone should be able to have you."

Derrick Jaxn

"At some point, you must stop giving all of you to people who only have pieces to offer in return."

Derrick Jaxn

"What catches your eye isn't always qualified to hold your heart."

Derrick Jaxn

CONGRATS!!!

You've officially completed the jump-start to a life of daily, unapologetic, and intentional self-love. The same way your body needs daily nutrition and your job requires regular attendance, your soul needs you to show up daily and even hourly with something to pour into it or protect it from.

The Self-Crowned Journal has guided you in that direction, given you the foundation you need, and now it's time for you to continue the rest of this journey on your own. If you were still growing from this set of daily tasks, feel free to grab another Self-Crowned Journal, or if you're ready for new areas to build in, write out a different curriculum for yourself to go by. But whatever you do, KEEP GOING!

This is not just a one-and-done thing. This must be a part of your life in order to keep your cup full. This is also a great time to add more resources to your tool belt. Think about the types of programs you can involve yourself in, new endeavors to embark on, new online or local groups to join, books to read, changes to your diet, places to travel, etc. that can keep you discovering ways to increasingly love yourself. Earnestly seek out those things, spaces, and relationships, and embrace them. You are officially self-crowned, and every step from this point forward is another precious jewel to represent your royalty.

CPSIA information can be obtained
at www.ICGtesting.com
Printed in the USA
FFHW010604221119
56111768-62196FF